Also by the Author

Black Magic

The Erin O'Reilly Mysteries
Book Six

Steven Henry

Clickworks Press • Baltimore, MD

First publication: Clickworks Press, 2019
Release: CWP-EOR6-INT-P.IS-1.0

Sign up for updates, deals, and exclusive sneak peeks at clickworkspress.com/join.

ISBN-10: 1-943383-55-3
ISBN-13: 978-1-943383-55-9

For Aunt Mary

Black Magic

Muddle 12 fresh red grapes in the base of a shaker. Add ½ ounce Grand Marnier Cordon Rouge Liqueur. Shake with ice and strain into chilled fluted glass. Top with champagne and serve.

- OR -

In a cocktail shaker, combine ½ cup orange juice and ½ ounce triple sec over ice. Shake well and strain into a glass. Layer 1 ½ ounces black vodka on top by pouring slowly over an upturned spoon. Garnish with an orange wedge with one end dipped in black vodka.

- OR -

In a cocktail shaker, combine 2 ½ ounces black vodka, ½ ounce simple syrup, and ¾ ounce fresh-squeezed lime juice over ice. Shake hard for 30 seconds. Add a dash of edible pearl dust to the bottom of a martini glass and strain cocktail into glass. Add more pearl dust and stir with a bar spoon for extra sparkle and shimmer.

- OR, to treat a hangover -

Empty two 260mg capsules of activated charcoal into a small bowl. Whisk together the charcoal and 1 ounce honey syrup. In a shaker, combine with 1 ¾ ounces fresh lime juice and 2 ¼ ounces fresh beet juice over ice. Shake and strain into a rocks glass filled with fresh ice. The mixture should be jet black.

Chapter 1

"Five! Four! Three!"

Erin O'Reilly braced herself. She tried to look confident. She remembered what her dad had told her.

When you're a cop, you always need to look like you're in control. Especially when you're not.

"Two! One!"

This was it. She took a deep breath.

"Happy New Year!"

She wasn't quite close enough to hear the roar from Times Square. She was watching the ball drop on her brother's TV set in his Midtown brownstone. Cars were honking their horns outside and people were cheering, all over the city.

Sean Junior put his arms around his wife, Michelle, and gave her a kiss.

"Eww," Anna said, hiding her face in her hands. Erin's niece had only just turned eight. She would think kisses gross for a few more years, thank God. Anna's little brother, Patrick, hadn't quite made it to midnight. He was curled up at one end of the couch, fast asleep in spite of the racket.

Erin turned to the guy she'd brought to their little New

Year's party. "How about it, partner? A kiss for good luck?" She bent over and brought her face close to his.

Rolf extended his tongue and licked her chin.

"Good boy," she said and rubbed her K-9 behind the ears. She wasn't feeling very celebratory, but spending the evening with her brother and his family beat drinking at home. And she'd been doing too much of that lately.

"You could've brought a date," Michelle said. She raised her champagne glass and clinked it against Sean's, then Erin's.

"Dogs are better company than boyfriends," Erin said.

"Says you," Michelle said, winking.

"Anna, back me up on this," Erin said. "Who would you rather have at a party? A boy, or Rolf?"

"Rolfie!" Anna said in tones of finality.

Erin shrugged. "I guess that's settled."

"Come on, Erin," Michelle persisted. "You can't not have a date on New Year's Eve!"

"God, Shelley. You're starting to sound like my mom."

Michelle smiled. "Are you working in a police station, or a convent?"

"What's a convent?" Anna asked.

"It's where I'll put you once the boys start sniffing around you," Sean said. "Ow!"

Michelle pretended she hadn't just shot her husband an elbow and kept looking at Erin.

"What?" Erin demanded.

Michelle raised an eyebrow and waited.

"Sis, I interrogate crooks for a living," Erin said. "I'm not gonna give you anything."

"So there is something," Michelle said triumphantly. "Okay, spill."

"No!"

"There must be a reason you don't want to tell me," Michelle said. "Let's see. Oh, I know! It's another cop. Maybe one your dad knows?"

Erin didn't want to play this game. "Think what you want," she said. "It's late, and I work in the morning. Vic's gonna be hung over, so I'll have to pick up his slack."

Michelle pouted a little. "Erin, something's been bothering you all season, and I'm guessing it's guy trouble. You were grumpy at Christmas."

"I was not!"

It was Michelle's turn to look to her family for support.

"I take the Fifth," Sean said, turning his attention to the TV.

"Fifth what?" asked Anna.

"Amendment," Erin said. "It's something people say when they're guilty but don't want to say so. And I was not grumpy!"

"Yes, you were," Anna said. "But it's okay, Aunt Erin. We love you anyway."

"She's right," Michelle said. "And you don't have to tell me now. But you should probably tell somebody, sometime. The job you do, it's not good to be distracted."

Erin didn't have an answer for that, because Michelle was right. She was distracted, it was guy trouble, and it was a problem. It'd been a little over two months since she'd let her emotions get the better of her judgment. As a result, she'd gotten too close to a man who was, to put it mildly, a risky relationship prospect. Morton Carlyle was handsome, charming, and witty. He was also a mid-level member of the Irish Mob, a career criminal, and a very dangerous man to associate with. Erin had spent the past ten weeks trying to forget their last encounter had happened. She hadn't succeeded.

Michelle was still watching her with sisterly concern.

It irritated Erin. "I've got plenty of worse things to worry about than whatever crazy ideas you've got about my love life," she said. "You do know my job involves people who kill other people, right?"

"That's true," Michelle said. "But I'm not qualified to give you advice on that part of your life."

Erin had to bite her tongue not to ask Michelle how being a stay-at-home mom qualified her to give advice on Erin's relationship status. "I really do need to get going," she said instead, draining the last of her champagne. "Thanks for having me over."

"No problem," Sean said, turning back toward her now that the girl talk seemed to be over. "Here, I'll give you a good-luck kiss." He planted a brotherly smack on her cheek.

"Me, too." Michelle followed up on Erin's other cheek. "You should come over more, Erin. Don't be such a stranger."

"Between my hours and hers, it's a wonder she and I even know we're still alive," Sean said. He was a trauma surgeon who worked long night shifts, and Erin was a detective with the NYPD's Major Crimes Division. "I just hope our professional lives stay separate."

"Me, too," Erin said. She got her jacket out of the hall closet. "Good night, Shelley, Sean, Anna. Hope this year is better than the last."

"Always," Sean said. "And I hope our jobs are boring and uneventful."

Erin's job stayed that way until she'd almost gotten back to her own apartment. Then her phone rang, and things got weird.

Chapter 2

"Where are you?" were the first words Lieutenant Webb said.

"South Manhattan," Erin replied.

"You sober?"

"Yeah. What's up?"

"Get to Midtown West right now. Theater District, Forty-Second Street."

"On my way." Erin's heart lurched. She was thinking of all the things that could go wrong in a crowded theater. Fire, gas leak, bomb, active shooter.

Her car was an unmarked black Charger with a special compartment for Rolf in the back. She put on the siren and low-profile flashers and sped up. In October she and her squad had barely managed to stop a terrorist from blowing up a big chunk of central Manhattan. What if they were too late this time? "I'm ten to fifteen out," she said. "What've we got?"

"One victim."

"Just one?" Erin was relieved but confused. "Why isn't Homicide handling it?"

"According to the responding officer, it's a strange one,"

Webb said. "Apparently our victim was cut in half."

"In half?"

"That's what I said."

"We got any witnesses?"

"Apparently about six hundred."

Erin wasn't sure she'd heard right. "Six hundred?"

"O'Reilly, this will be a long conversation if you repeat everything I say."

"What happened?"

"We're going to figure that out. It's our job, being detectives and all. Sounds like an actress got chopped up on stage, in the middle of a performance."

"Jesus."

"I don't think so, but it's a little early to rule out any suspects," Webb said dryly. "I'm just about on site. Neshenko's on his way. See you in a few."

*　　*　　*

Broadway was packed with over forty theaters, but it wasn't hard to tell which one was the crime scene. Half a dozen squad cars were out front, their blue-and-red flashers competing with the marquee lights. The sign over the theater proclaimed THE GREAT RONALDO'S PHANTASMAGORIA in blood-red letters. Big posters on either side of the entrance depicted a mysterious black-cloaked figure standing behind a screaming woman strapped to a table while a buzz-saw chewed through the wood. Under the circumstances, Erin found the posters in bad taste.

She parked with the rest of the police vehicles, retrieved Rolf from the back seat, showed her gold shield to the uniformed officers at the door, and went inside.

It was the busiest crime scene she'd ever investigated.

People were everywhere. Most were in evening attire, suit coats and ties for the men, dresses for the women. Even the kids, and she was sorry to see a fair number, had on button-down shirts and cute dresses. Most of the kids, and more than a few adults, were crying. Others had stunned, shocked expressions on their faces and stared straight through whatever their eyes were pointed at. Erin had seen that look before, on survivors of car accidents and shootings.

A bunch of uniforms were doing their best to keep everyone in order, but there weren't nearly enough cops on scene. Erin's instinct was to pitch in and help. But she was a detective, and crowd control wasn't her job. She worked her way through the lobby and into the auditorium.

Lieutenant Webb and Vic Neshenko were on the stage in front of the curtain. They were talking to a tall, thin man in a tuxedo and cape; presumably, the Great Ronaldo. The curtain had been drawn down by some quick-thinking stagehand, so the crime scene wasn't visible to the audience, but Erin could see a garish fan of blood-spatter.

She and Rolf made it down to the front rows. The crowd thinned out here, and it wasn't hard to guess why. Blood had splattered clean into the fourth row. She saw stains on the upholstery, on the floor, just about everywhere. The most disturbing thing was, several seat-backs had clean patches in the center, outlining where people had been sitting.

Erin planted her hands on the edge of the stage, careful to avoid the bloody patch, and levered herself up. Rolf leaped and scrambled up beside her. The two of them approached the other two detectives. Vic's eyes were bloodshot and he looked about thirty percent drunk. She smelled liquor on Webb's breath, too, but he didn't show any outward sign of intoxication.

"O'Reilly," Webb said. "Glad you're here. This is Ronald Whitaker, otherwise known as the Great Ronaldo."

The tall man made a slight bow and smiled thinly. He'd tried to wipe his face clean, but little spots of blood were visible around his eyebrows and his neat little black mustache and goatee.

"What happened?" Erin asked.

"If you wouldn't mind going over it again," Webb said to the magician. "From the beginning?"

"Yes, of course," The Great Ronaldo said. "We were doing our show, everything was going great. The crowd was really engaged. You can feel it, when the house is with you. It's an electric kind of thing, something special. Kat had a real spark to her tonight."

"Excuse me," Erin said. "Kat?"

"My assistant," he explained. "Katarzyna the Gypsy."

"That her real name?" Vic asked.

"No, that's a professional name. She's Kathy... Kathy Grimes."

"Go on," Webb said. He looked tired, too, but Webb always looked tired. Erin had never seen him without bags under his eyes.

"We'd just finished the knife-throwing, where Kat gets tied to a target and I toss knives all around her. Those are real knives, sharp ones."

"Sounds dangerous," Erin said.

The magician shrugged. "No trickery there, nothing fancy. Just hours and hours of practice. I can throw a knife blindfolded and I won't hit something unless I mean to."

"You were saying?" Webb prompted.

"We were all set for one of the big numbers, the table saw," Ronaldo went on. "I tied her down, we got it running, and something went wrong."

"Hold it," Vic said. "That isn't a real power saw, is it?" He jerked a thumb over his shoulder toward the curtain.

"Yes, it is," Ronaldo said. "That's part of the effect. We cut through a few things just beforehand, to prove it's a real blade. For dramatic effect, building the tension."

"But you don't actually cut the girl in half," Vic observed. "Usually."

Ronaldo shook his head. "No, that's never happened before."

"We're going to need you to show us how the trick is supposed to work," Webb said.

"I can't do that."

"Why not, exactly?"

"A magician can't demonstrate his tricks to anyone, especially a non-magician."

Webb took a deep breath and looked at the ceiling for a moment. If he was looking for patience, he didn't find it there. "Mr. Whitaker," he said, returning his gaze to the man, "this is a homicide investigation. Either we're looking at a terrible accident, or premeditated murder. The amount of trouble you're in will only increase if you don't cooperate. We're going to examine the device. Your choice is whether we do it with your permission, or without it."

Ronaldo sighed. "May I rely on your professional courtesy and discretion, Detective?"

"Absolutely."

"Let's have a look at this thing," Vic said.

* * *

Police officers saw a lot of death. It came with the job. As a first responder, Erin had come face to face with dead bodies at car accidents, in apartments, in back alleys. Everywhere people lived, people could die. Every cop learned to put on emotional armor, or else they burned out fast.

But sometimes a really bad scene pierced the armor.

Erin felt it like a physical blow. When they saw the apparatus, and what had happened to Kathy Grimes, the three detectives just stood there. None of them said anything. None of them moved. Time stopped for a little while. Erin couldn't hear the chattering audience members on the other side of the curtain. Her vision went dark at the corners. For a second, she genuinely thought she might faint.

Vic finally broke the silence. "Shit," he said in a calm, thoughtful tone.

Webb sighed and adjusted his necktie. He didn't give any outward sign of being upset. If anything, he just looked a little more tired. "Levine's on the way," he said.

"The hell for?" Vic demanded. "Cause of death? Pretty goddamn obvious."

"Can it," Erin snapped.

Vic looked at her in surprise. "What?"

"This is bad enough without your attitude," she said. She'd have a hard time explaining it, but she was suddenly finding him irritating.

"What'd I say?" he shot back.

"Both of you, quiet," Webb said softly. "I want the ME's report before we move the body."

"Which half?" Vic replied.

Erin tried to think objectively. This wasn't the first time she'd seen a gruesome body. Hell, some highway accidents were as bad as this, or worse. She'd seen severed limbs thrown out of cars, corpses burned to a crisp. There wasn't anything special about this.

Maybe it was the way it'd happened. A young woman had been cut to pieces in front of hundreds of people, and no one had stopped it happening. Not even the man who'd been standing right there.

She turned away from the horrible sight and faced The

Great Ronaldo. "Why didn't you do something?" she demanded.

"Like what?" Ronaldo sounded surprised.

"Like stop the damn saw!"

"It happened so fast," he said. "It's never happened that way before."

Erin wanted to punch him. If he'd reacted properly, just maybe the victim could've been saved.

"How does this work?" Webb asked. "You said it was a real saw blade."

"That's right," the magician said. He took a deep breath. Apparently, giving up one of his tricks bothered him as much as having his assistant bisected in front of him. "There's a lever there, on the back of the apparatus."

"This?" Vic gingerly stepped around pools of blood and poked the toe of his shoe at a well-concealed section of machinery, being careful not to touch anything.

"That's it," Ronaldo said. "But when I pressed it, nothing happened."

"That's the only thing that keeps you from turning a girl into cold cuts?" Vic said in disbelief.

Erin gritted her teeth.

"There's a backup safety catch," Ronaldo said. "A locking pin engages and guides the blade onto a lower track. The blade slides under the table while a pyrotechnic effect creates a shower of sparks and smoke."

Vic bent down to look under the machine. "Doesn't look like there's room."

"There's a mirror," Ronaldo explained. "It uses forced perspective to make the blade appear to run on its original track. It appears to be passing directly through the assistant."

Vic moved his head from side to side, trying to make it out. "Okay," he said doubtfully. He rapped his knuckles on the glass under the slab to make sure it was real and solid.

"But the locking pin didn't engage," Ronaldo said. "I'm not sure why."

"You test this equipment before the show?" Webb asked.

"Yes," Ronaldo said. "Something must have gone wrong."

"Obviously," Webb said dryly.

Out of the corner of her eye, Erin saw a new arrival come onto the stage. For a moment, she didn't recognize her; a slender brunette in a black evening dress with a glamorous hairdo.

Then the woman walked briskly forward and peered at the ghastly scene with professional interest, pulling a pair of rubber gloves out of her handbag. "Give me some room," she said.

Vic and Erin did a simultaneous double-take. "Levine?" they echoed one another.

Sarah Levine, Precinct 8's Medical Examiner, nodded absently.

"You look... good," Vic managed to get out. To the best of Erin's knowledge, no one at the Eightball had ever seen Levine in anything but a lab coat, surgical scrubs, and the most basic hairstyle.

"I didn't have time to change," Levine answered without looking at him.

"Must've been a hell of a party," Vic said. "Sorry we called you out before—"

Levine didn't even let him finish. "Victim is a Caucasian female, aged early twenties. No lividity or rigor. Probably less than an hour since TOD, definitely less than two."

"We've got time of death," Webb said. "Pretty much to the second."

Levine kept talking without looking up. "Blood spatter indicates a living body. We have definite arterial bleeding from the lower body. Initial cause of death appears to be lateral traumatic bisection of the pelvic region and abdomen, beginning in the pelvic region and ending above the left shoulder. By the time the blade transited the thoracic cavity, the damage was already mortal. However, you can see from the spatter pattern that the heartbeat did not entirely cease until the heart itself was bisected."

"Jesus," Vic muttered. "We get the picture."

"The blade continued its transit, but did not contact the cranium," she went on, "likely due to muscular contractions at the moment of death. The blade exited the body just above the left scapula, bisecting the clavicle. I'll need samples for the bloodwork, of course."

"That shouldn't present a problem," Webb said with quiet understatement. "Where's CSU?"

"Getting their gear," Levine said. "The team from the morgue is here, too."

"Oh, no," Erin said. "Not them."

As if on cue, the two guys from the coroner's van showed up in the wings. They couldn't move the body until the Crime Scene Unit took pictures, but they apparently had nothing better to do than hang around until then. Ernie was the tall, thin one and Hank was the short, stocky one. They had a knack for saying the absolute worst possible things.

She was in no mood to deal with their bullshit, not with something that horrible right next to her. "Not a word," she said, taking a threatening step toward them.

Hank spread his hands, the picture of innocence.

Ernie, staring at the scene, was quietly singing. "Take time with a wounded hand 'cause it likes to heal, I like to steal... I'm half the man I used to be..."

Hank joined in. "This feeling as the dawn it turns to gray..."

"Well, I'm half the man I used to be," Ernie went on.

Vic caught Erin's wrist, spoiling the fist she was getting ready to launch into Ernie's jaw. "Hey," he said. "Don't."

She spun around. "Let go," she growled.

Rolf, picking up on her mood, started a low rumble in his chest. His hackles went up. He liked Vic, but he wasn't about to let anyone manhandle his partner.

Vic let his hand drop. Then he turned to the two guys who drove the meat wagon. "And if you two assholes don't shut it, I won't stop her next time. Hell, I'll join in."

Ernie grinned, but he trailed off into silence.

"What're you talking about?" Hank asked. "It was just our halftime show..."

Erin moved too fast for Vic this time. She didn't punch Hank. She used an open hand and shoved his shoulder, spinning the little guy almost halfway around. Then she walked off the stage into the wings, found a dark corner, and put her hands over her face. She was trembling with adrenaline, anger, and residual shock.

Rolf nosed cautiously at her. He wagged his tail and stared with his serious brown eyes.

She rubbed his ears without really thinking about it. After a while, she felt a little bit better. But she knew, no matter when she got to bed, sleep would be a long time coming. What the hell was the matter with her?

Chapter 3

The sky was just getting light when Erin dragged herself into her apartment. Webb had sent her and Vic home to catch a little rest. The Lieutenant was still at the theater, overseeing a bunch of uniforms and taking an endless stream of witness statements. For a burned-out old veteran, Webb had an awful lot of stamina.

Rolf hopped up on her bed, curled into a ball, and went to sleep. Erin took off her Glock and gold shield and laid them on the nightstand. Then she went back to the kitchen, where the liquor cabinet was waiting for her.

The whiskey was a micro-brand called Glen Docherty-Kinlochewe. Since no one west of the Atlantic knew how to pronounce that, it went by the abbreviation Glen D. She hardly glanced at the beautiful, transparent amber fluid as she poured herself a double shot. It was high-quality liquor and went down easy.

The first drink took the edge off her anger. She paused for a moment in the act of refilling her glass. The Glen D was running pretty low. This was her last bottle, and it was less than a quarter full. That was a problem. Her supply had dried up.

Glen D was an exclusive import of an Irish organization, specifically, the O'Malley crime family. She'd had a great line on as much of the good stuff as she could drink, free of charge, ever since she'd saved Carlyle's pub from getting blown to bits. But she'd screwed that up.

Maybe it was just as well to go back to drinking Jameson, she thought morosely. The Glen D tasted like Carlyle. So smooth, with that hint of exotic foreign flavor. A girl could get drunk on it without even noticing.

She curled her hand into a fist around her glass and poured the second drink. Carlyle had called her cell phone eight times, without getting an answer, until she'd blocked his number. Of course, being Carlyle, he hadn't let that stop him. He'd gone to a burner cell. The unknown number on her caller ID had gotten him as far as her saying "O'Reilly." The moment she heard his voice, she'd hung up on him and blocked that number, too.

He'd gotten the message and hadn't tried to contact her again. Carlyle wasn't the kind of guy who'd keep throwing himself at someone. He had his pride. But so did she, damn it.

How could she have let herself be so careless? She was a detective with the NYPD. He was a mid-level mob boss. Who he was didn't matter. What he was, that was the issue. Maybe he'd been using her the whole time, playing a long game, getting closer. Grooming her. Or maybe he really had fallen for her. But that wasn't the point.

The point was that Erin had been trying to block out what had happened for two and a half months. Fortunately, she had her work to keep her mind occupied. And when the work ended, she had her cache of Glen D.

"For a little longer, at least," she muttered, glaring at the almost-empty bottle. She was feeling the comfortable, warm numbness starting to spread out from her stomach. Maybe she'd be able to get some sleep after all.

*   *   *

Erin woke up with her head pounding. She rolled over, groaned, looked at the clock, and groaned again. She still didn't know whether they were investigating a terrible accident or a homicide, but either way, it was time to get on it. She pulled herself out of bed.

Rolf was a lot perkier than she was, probably because she hadn't given him any whiskey. He was up and alert, eager for their morning run.

She didn't want to go. Hangovers and cardio didn't mix, and it was way too cold out. But force of habit got her into a set of NYPD sweats and out the door.

It was a bright, sunny January day. The light drove spikes of pain straight up her optic nerves into her brain. Every running footstep jarred up her spine. But she kept going, ignoring the pain, running through it. By the time she got back to her apartment, sweat soaking into her clothes, her head was a little clearer.

As she climbed the steps to the front door, she paused. Something tugged at her Patrol instincts. She had the feeling someone was watching. She turned and gave a quick scan to her surroundings. The apartment fronted on a small park across the street. She saw a few pedestrians, some passing cars, but nothing out of the ordinary.

Erin shook her head. She'd been ambushed by Russian hitmen, stalked by a serial killer, and shot at more than once. That was no excuse for being paranoid. If she started imagining dangers outside her door, she'd never leave her apartment. She went inside to grab a quick shower before heading to work.

*   *   *

Webb had beaten her to the Precinct 8 Major Crimes office. He didn't look any worse than he had the night before. He didn't look any better, either. Erin imagined she didn't look so good either. She hadn't slept nearly enough.

"Morning," Webb said, without offering any opinion on whether it was a good one or not.

"Morning, sir," she said. "Where's Vic?"

"Still asleep," Webb said. "Or maybe dead."

"Speaking of which…" Erin prompted.

Webb pointed to the department's whiteboard. He'd put up pictures of Kathy Grimes and Ronald Whitaker that he'd clipped out of a theater program. Whitaker was listed under "Suspects."

"So, homicide?" she asked.

He nodded. "A couple of our tech guys took the machine apart overnight. I just saw their report. The device was sabotaged."

"They're sure it wasn't an accident?"

"A chain link was filed through and the gap filled with wax," he explained, picking up a folder from his desk and flipping through it. "CSU found the residue. Someone wanted it to pass inspection. The magician, Whitaker, said they ran the saw a couple minutes before doing the trick. But running the motor created heat, which softened the wax. Then the chain parted and you can guess how things went from there."

"Ouch," Erin said.

"So, we need to find out who wanted to kill Kathy Grimes," he said. "Specifically, someone who wanted to kill her publicly and horribly, and was willing to go to considerable lengths to make that happen. Then we need to figure who on that list had access to the machinery and the knowhow to set it up."

"The Great Ronaldo, of course," she said.

"What about him?" Vic asked from the stairwell.

"Damn," Erin said. "You look like I feel."

Vic took a long pull from the gigantic soda cup in his hand. Erin knew better than to ask what was in it.

"Whitaker's our only suspect so far," Webb said. "He certainly understood the device. He and Grimes worked together, so there could be any number of reasons he might want to kill her."

"Yeah," Vic said. "Except that he'd have to be a total moron. Think about it, Lieutenant. What sort of oxygen thief decides to kill a woman in front of six hundred witnesses, every one of which is guaranteed to be looking right at him while he does it? Hell, we've even got a couple videos of it happening off smartphones, don't we?"

"We do," Webb sighed. "I'm not used to having too many eyewitnesses."

"How many did you talk to?" Erin asked.

"Enough. For once, pretty much all the accounts agree. It's like music. Get enough people singing together, it averages out on key."

"So what do we do now?" Vic asked.

"Our jobs," Webb said. "Erin, you do background on Grimes. Find out who she was, what made her tick. I got some info from Whitaker, but it'll need to be verified. The file's on your desk, along with emergency contact info. She had parents in Detroit."

"Family notification?" Erin asked, her heart sinking. It was one of the worst parts of the Job.

He nodded. "Someone has to. Neshenko?"

"Yeah?"

"I want a list of everyone who works at the theater. Whether they were on the clock during the show or not. Ushers, stagehands, concessions, everyone."

"I miss Kira," Vic muttered. "She actually likes this shit."

"Excuse me?" Webb inquired politely. "I may have misheard you, but I think you just said something about requesting a transfer to permanent traffic duty?"

Vic twitched but didn't say anything. He went to his desk and sat down heavily.

Erin took a seat at her own desk with about as much enthusiasm. She missed Kira Jones, too. They hadn't seen much of her since Kira had transferred to Internal Affairs at the end of their last big case. Erin had the feeling the other woman was avoiding her old colleagues. It was a real shame, especially when there was research to be done. Kira was a master at wading through data.

Erin looked at the Kathy Grimes folder. The top sheet had the names Bernard and Loretta Grimes and a phone number. She was about to dial when she remembered Webb had said they were from Detroit, where it was an hour earlier. She'd be ruining their day no matter what, but she could at least let them wake up first. She set the phone number aside and started running computer checks on the victim.

Some interesting things turned up when she did a search on the National Crime Information Center database. A Kathy Grimes had pled out on a burglary charge in Detroit four years ago. The same person had gone to trial for grand larceny but had been acquitted. Apparently, she'd been accused of stealing from a low-level manager at General Motors the year before her burglary bust. Erin wasn't sure whether any of that was pertinent, but figured she'd better add it to the file. Maybe someone Grimes had ripped off had decided to go outside the law to get even. She found a few other hits on the name, scattered around the country, but they might just be people sharing a name.

Then it was time to make the phone call. Erin took a deep breath and dialed Detroit.

She'd just about resigned herself to leaving a voicemail, but someone picked up on the fourth ring. A noncommittal male voice came on the line.

"Yeah?"

"Sir," she said, "I'm trying to reach Mr. and Mrs. Grimes. My name is Erin O'Reilly. I'm a detective with the New York Police Department."

There was a pause. "You got the wrong Grimes," the guy on the other end said. "Don't you guys check your area codes? I'm in friggin' Detroit."

"Are you Bernard Grimes, the father of Kathy Grimes?"

There was another pause. "Yeah," he said cautiously. "What's going on? What'd Kat do now? Do I need to bring a lawyer in on this? Christ, you know how much that girl's cost us, legal fees alone?"

Erin closed her eyes. "Mr. Grimes, I'm sorry to have to tell you this. There was an... incident at the magic show last night. One of the stage props malfunctioned. I'm afraid Kathy was killed."

"What?"

"I'm sorry," she said again. "Kathy was killed, pretty much instantly." That was a lie, but a comforting one.

"Are you sure?"

"Sir?"

"Are... are you sure it's her?"

"She was identified by her employer, Mr. Whitaker," Erin said. "We also have a fingerprint confirmation from..."

"From her criminal record," Mr. Grimes sighed. He sounded like he'd just taken a pretty hard hit to the stomach. "This is gonna break Loretta's heart. I didn't mean it, what I just said.

We do love that girl, no matter how much crap she put us through."

"Mr. Grimes? I'm sorry to ask this, but do you know anyone who might have had a reason to hurt Kathy?"

"I... I don't understand. I thought you said there was an accident."

"It's being investigated as a homicide, sir."

"How... how did she..." He couldn't finish the question.

"Do you know what Kathy's job was?" she asked, looking for a way to avoid answering that. There were some details Kathy's parents really did not want to know.

"Yeah. She works for that magician, helping him with his magic tricks."

"What do you know about her work?"

"We went to see her once, when they were in Detroit." Mr. Grimes's voice took on a heavy layer of disgust.

"Only the once?"

"Back before I was married, I went out to a club once with some of the guys," he said. "I saw goddamn strippers wearing more clothes than my daughter had on that stage. I couldn't believe it. It was the most humiliating moment of my life. Yeah, even worse than seeing her in court. Of course I didn't go see her again."

Erin wasn't quite sure where to go from there. "I'm sorry," she said for what felt like the tenth time in the conversation. "Were you in close contact with your daughter?"

"No." Now Mr. Grimes just sounded worn out. "We had an argument after that show. I told her what I thought of her job. I was pissed off and I let her know it. She blew up and told me that at least she had a job. I was laid off, see. Been out of work the last couple years, living off unemployment. I used to work the line for General Motors. The job went overseas. You know how it is."

"Do you know if she knew anyone in New York?"

"She said something to Loretta about a new boyfriend, I think."

Erin's heart jumped. "Do you know his name?"

"No. She wasn't talking to me."

"Can I speak with Loretta, please?"

"She's at work."

"Would you please have her call me as soon as possible?"

"Yeah, of course." Mr. Grimes cleared his throat. "Uh, Detective, I don't really know what we're supposed to do now. Do you need us to come out there? Or can someone ship the, uh... How does this work, anyway?"

"We've got a victim-assistance coordinator," Erin said. "I'll put you in touch with their office. They'll help you through the process."

They stumbled through the rest of the call, exchanging the necessary contact info. Mr. Grimes wanted to know more, but there wasn't much she could tell him, and what she did know, she was sure he didn't want to hear. When the call ended, she was left wondering whether Kathy Grimes's death had been more of a tragedy or a nuisance for him.

Her mood wasn't improved by the next thing on her plate. She had to go down to the morgue to get the preliminary report from the Medical Examiner. It was a good thing to do before noon. Better to lose her appetite than her lunch.

It wasn't the gruesome sights that got to Erin; it was the smells. The mix of lab chemicals and death was uniquely awful. Sometimes the cops on TV used Vicks Vaporub to kill the stink, but that didn't really work. There was nothing on Earth you could put under your nose to keep out the smell of a dead body. You just had to get used to it.

Levine was living proof that it was possible to deal with the stink. She'd obviously been there all night. She'd changed out of her New Year's dress into her scrubs and lab coat, but she hadn't bothered to take her hair out of its fancy styling or wash off her makeup. It made for a strange visual.

"So, what'd they drag you away from last night?" Erin asked.

Levine looked blank.

Erin reminded herself that the other woman considered it her true calling to examine bodies. She might just as well have asked Levine if getting invited to parties ever dragged her away from crime scenes. "Where were you when you got the call?" she tried instead. "You said it was a party. What kind of thing?"

"Oh. I was out with Jasper."

Erin let that sit for a few moments, waiting for Levine to elaborate, then gave up. "Who's Jasper?"

"My fiancé."

"I didn't know you were engaged."

Levine didn't say anything.

"So," Erin said when she felt the silence becoming uncomfortable. "What've you got on the Grimes woman?"

"The bloodwork came back clean," Levine said. "No drugs, toxins, or alcohol. Cause of death was longitudinal bisection of the abdomen and thorax, as anticipated. The autopsy was somewhat simplified due to the nature of the injury, as the standard Y-incision was redundant." She gestured toward the table.

Erin really didn't want to look. She gave it as brief a glance as she felt she could get away with. "Yeah, I get it."

"The procedure was straightforward," Levine went on. "I didn't notice anything out of place. There was some bruising around the wrists and ankles, but I consider that to be due to the restraints I observed on the victim's extremities at the scene."

"She tried to pull loose," Erin said quietly. "When she realized what was happening." She swallowed. "How long did it take?"

"The massive drop in blood pressure would have caused rapid shock," Levine said. "I expect the victim lost consciousness in a matter of no more than twenty seconds, probably less."

"Anything else?"

"I swabbed the wound and found some foreign matter, but it appears to have been introduced during the incident." Levine shrugged. "This wasn't a mysterious death. She died exactly the way it looked."

"Right, thanks," Erin said and got out of there. The smell was getting harder to bear.

Chapter 4

As expected, visiting the morgue had pretty much killed Erin's appetite, but she still wanted to get out of the precinct at lunchtime. The brisk January air was a nice change from the stuffy Major Crimes office, and definitely an improvement over the blood and formaldehyde in the basement. She took Rolf for a walk while she tried to think.

She kept remembering the scene on the theater stage, kept imagining what those last moments must have been like for Kathy Grimes. One minute it was all fun and games, a magic trick; the next, she was dying in front of hundreds of people, and by the time anyone realized what was happening, it was already too late. Who the hell could do such a thing?

Erin was a career cop who'd spent eleven years working Patrol before earning her gold shield. She had good instincts that had kept her alive. It was an indicator of how preoccupied she was that she'd gone a good block and a half from the precinct before she realized she was being followed.

In fairness, it wasn't that obvious. Downtown Manhattan at noon was full of people, even on New Year's Day, with half the populace nursing hangovers and catching up on sleep. Erin was just one of hundreds of pedestrians on the street. At least half a dozen other dogs were getting lunchtime walks within view. And that wasn't even taking into account the cars, taxis, and delivery trucks on the street.

Still, she was being followed. She knew it with the sudden tingle on the back of her neck that every good street officer learned not to ignore.

Erin didn't panic. She unzipped her jacket, in spite of the cold, so she could get to her Glock in a hurry if she needed it. She shifted her hand on Rolf's leash. She could turn him loose with a single quick flick and a word.

Then she started working her environment. One of the assets of being in an urban setting was all the reflective surfaces. Shop windows were best, but parked cars had windows and rear-view mirrors. She started using them to check behind her, making sure to keep her motions casual, trying to catch a glimpse of her shadow.

Until she made him, she was still wondering if she was just indulging her paranoia. But then she saw the man and recognized him.

She'd seen him once or twice before. He was O'Malley muscle. He'd been one of Carlyle's bodyguards, and it couldn't possibly be a coincidence that he was walking down the same Manhattan street she was, keeping within about twenty yards of her.

Now that she'd seen him, Erin decided it was about time to turn the tables on these Irish Mob goons. When she got to the next corner, she turned, took a few steps, then spun around and came right back. She'd timed it well. Her tail was less than ten feet from her and coming on fast. They made eye contact.

He had a hard face, with a military buzz-cut that showed a thin scar just over one ear. He wasn't much taller than Erin and almost as lightly built, but he looked dangerous. His eyes were calm, almost expressionless. Killer's eyes.

He paused. Then he quietly said, "Excuse me, ma'am," and started walking around her.

Erin looked at his hands. They were empty and in plain view, which was good. "Hold on," she said, sidestepping to block him. A couple of New Yorkers hesitated, glancing at them, but most of the bystanders kept on about their business.

He stopped. "Yes, ma'am?" He seemed completely relaxed. That was either a good sign, or a very bad one.

Erin didn't know quite what to say. She fell back on a line from a movie. "How about I buy you a cup of coffee?"

He finally looked startled. Then he gave her just a hint of a smile. She realized he was younger than she'd thought, mid-twenties at the oldest. "That'd be nice, ma'am."

In downtown Manhattan it was hard to be more than a couple hundred yards from a coffee shop. She led the way to the closest one, keeping an eye on him just in case. He wasn't making any aggressive moves, but she knew better than to turn her back. Once inside, she flashed her shield to the barista, ensuring she'd have no trouble about Rolf. Erin ordered a cup of coffee, cream with no sugar. Her companion took his black. She found a two-person table by the window. Rolf sat beside Erin and kept an eye on the guy.

"So," she said. "You got a name?"

"Thompson, ma'am. Ian Thompson."

"You're former military, aren't you." The haircut, the way he talked, the scars, all pointed to it.

"Yes, ma'am. Marine Corps."

"What'd you do in the Corps?"

"Scout Sniper, ma'am. Sergeant."

"What're you doing working for Carlyle?"

If that surprised him, he didn't show it. "My job, ma'am."

"And you're riding my ass. Is that for my protection, or Carlyle's?"

Ian took a sip of his coffee. "Making sure you're okay, ma'am. I didn't intend to interfere. No excuse, ma'am."

Erin stared at him. "What are you, a babysitter?"

"No, ma'am."

"What, exactly, is your relationship with Morton Carlyle?"

"He's my employer."

She was surprised to hear him admit it. Most mob associates would deny connection with other wise guys. "What's your job description?"

"Personal security, ma'am. Bodyguard."

"Then why aren't you guarding him?"

"I'm on special assignment."

"You carrying?"

"Yes, ma'am."

"You got a permit?"

"Yes, ma'am. Unrestricted Concealed Carry."

"Bullshit." Pretty much the only people who got that kind of permit in New York City were cops, or retired cops. Even the National Guard couldn't carry guns off-duty in Erin's city.

"I have the permit, ma'am," Ian said. "Want to see it?"

"Yeah. Careful." Erin's hand went inside her jacket to rest next to her Glock.

Ian slowly took out his wallet and pulled the paperwork, handing it across the table. Erin scanned it. It looked legitimate.

"What are you carrying?" she asked.

"Beretta 92. What do you carry, ma'am?"

"Glock nine-millimeter," Erin said, too surprised to say anything but the truth.

"That's a good gun," Ian said. "And this is good coffee. Thank you, ma'am."

"You can earn it by telling Carlyle something for me."

"What's that, ma'am?"

Erin gritted her teeth. "Tell him I don't need a goddamn babysitter. I don't need his goons tripping over me. If he's got something he wants to say to me, he knows where I am. Otherwise, tell him to stay the hell out of my way."

Ian didn't flinch. Erin noticed more scars on his knuckles where his fingers were wrapped around his coffee cup. "I'll tell him what you said, ma'am," he said calmly. "But Mr. Carlyle's worried. I think..."

"What?"

Ian looked straight into her eyes. "He'd like to make things right."

Erin stood up. "Then that's on him, not you. So if you keep following me, Ian, I'll assume you're stalking me. Which is, of course, a felony."

Ian stood up. "You won't see me, ma'am. Thank you again for the coffee." Then he walked out of the coffee shop and disappeared into the Manhattan crowd.

*   *   *

"What happened to you?" Vic asked.

"Nothing," Erin said. She checked the break room and found half a glazed donut, only a little stale. She took it, went across the office to her desk, and dropped into her chair. Rolf took up his usual place on his carpet square next to her.

"Bullshit. What's wrong?" He spun his chair to face hers.

"What makes you think anything's wrong?"

"For starters, people who're fine never say that."

Erin wanted to slug him. "Before I said that," she growled.

"You checked your six when you came in the door."

"Like hell I did." But he was right. She'd reflexively glanced over her shoulder to see if anyone was following.

"Whatever." Vic shrugged and turned back to his desk, pretending not to care.

"Where's Webb?" she asked.

"Talking to Whitaker again."

"What do we do till he gets back?"

"Wipe out street crime in Manhattan. Got any suggestions?"

"Just the two of us? I say we wait for the ice caps to melt and flood all the streets."

"Wouldn't work," Vic said. "Venice has street crime, I'll bet."

"Gondola hijackings?"

"I want to deal with that shit, I'll join the Harbor Patrol," he said. "Right now, I'm studying machinery. Trying to figure out who might be able to rig up a stunt like they did on that power saw."

"I guess I'll keep digging on the victim," she said.

But that turned out to be a lie. Erin tried to work on the case, but she kept thinking about Carlyle and the O'Malleys. After trying and failing to put it out of her mind, she pulled up Ian Thompson's records.

Ian was twenty-six and came from Queens, just a few blocks from the house where Erin had grown up. She found an obit for his mom and arrest reports for his dad, a whole slew of DUIs and disorderly conduct collars. It was a typical sort of background for a mob associate. Happy families didn't tend to produce mobsters.

What was surprising was what she didn't find. Ian's record was a total blank from age thirteen to eighteen. As a general rule, if a guy was connected to organized crime, he'd done some jail time. The most unusual thing about Carlyle was that he'd never been arrested in the United States. Every one of his associates had been busted for something... except Ian

Thompson. The only thing she was able to dig up on him was some piddling juvenile-delinquent stuff. When he'd been twelve, he'd beaten up a couple other kids in a playground fight that'd left one in the hospital with a greenstick fracture.

The juvenile record had been sealed when he turned eighteen, of course, but something most people didn't realize was that law-enforcement officers could still get at sealed records. The protection was for employment applications, housing, that sort of thing. If he'd been arrested for anything at all, it'd be in the database, and it wasn't. Either he'd been a regular choirboy for five years straight, or someone had illegally scrubbed the records.

Erin frowned and kept looking. She moved on to his military records at the National Archives. He'd been telling the truth about the Marine Corps. He'd been inducted just after his high-school graduation and done a tour in Iraq right out of boot camp. That deployment earned him a bronze star and a promotion to corporal. When he'd gotten back to the States, he'd volunteered for Scout Sniper training. Then he'd gone on another tour, to Afghanistan this time. She didn't find much detail on that, but there was one thing that grabbed her attention.

"What've you got there?"

Erin jumped. She hadn't noticed Webb come in. She fought the guilty urge to shut the database window. "Got some background on a mob guy," she said.

"Wait a second," Webb said. "You think Grimes was a mob hit?"

"No, but I ran into this kinda shady guy over lunch," she said. "I wanted to check him out."

"Well, let's have a look," the Lieutenant said, coming around her desk. He started reading out loud. "The President of the United States takes pleasure in presenting the Silver Star Medal to Ian F. Thompson, Sergeant, U.S. Marine Corps, for conspicuous gallantry and intrepidity in action against the enemy as a Scout Sniper..." He looked up. "This guy's a hero, O'Reilly. You sure he's mobbed up?"

"I'm sure."

Webb looked back at the screen. "Following the destruction of his squad's helicopter during a nighttime operation in Kandahar Province," he continued, "Sergeant Thompson rescued a badly wounded fellow Marine. Pursued by a force of at least thirty enemy combatants, and assisting his wounded comrade, Sergeant Thompson successfully evaded the enemy and, over the following four days, crossed over one hundred kilometers of enemy-occupied territory on foot, engaging the enemy on two separate occasions and inflicting an estimated thirteen enemy casualties. Sergeant Thompson had virtually no ammunition, supplies, or rest during this time. Sergeant Thompson saved his fellow Marine's life. His courage, dedication to duty, and determination were in keeping with the highest traditions of the United States Naval Service."

"Damn," Vic said. "You met this guy?"

"Yeah," Erin said, sitting back and staring at her computer.

"You want some advice? Don't piss him off."

"Yeah," she said again, wondering why a man like that would be working for Carlyle, and why Carlyle had ordered him to keep an eye on her.

"Well, now you've looked up the guy you met on your lunch break," Webb said. "If you'd care to do some actual detective work, the Great Ronaldo has given us a suspect."

"Who?" Erin asked.

"The Amazing Lucien."

"Seriously?" Vic asked. "Did we step into a bad comic book?"

"Apparently he has the other big magic act in town," Webb said dryly. "He and Whitaker don't get along."

"So he saws up Whitaker's assistant?" Erin asked. "I don't buy it."

"It seems the victim was romantically involved with Lucien," Webb explained.

"That's more promising," she agreed. "Her dad told me she had a boyfriend, but he didn't have a name for me."

"Let's go talk to him," Webb said. "Neshenko, mind the shop here."

Vic sighed. "Sure thing, boss. Do I get any time off for good behavior?"

"That depends," Erin couldn't resist saying. "Have you ever done anything that qualifies as good behavior?"

Chapter 5

"I bet that's not hurting our guy's business any," Erin said. The Amazing Lucien was performing at the theater directly across the street from The Great Ronaldo's venue. She and Webb could see the police tape on the entrance to the other building.

"They're not the only two shows in town," Webb said. "But that's another motive, yeah. Taking out the competition."

"You think Whitaker's ever gonna go back on the stage?" Erin asked.

Webb snorted. "Even if he gets out of the legal trouble, the insurance premiums would kill him."

"Lucien's here?" Erin asked as they arrived at the theater door. "His show doesn't start until evening."

"I called his hotel," Webb said. "This is where they said he'd be." He opened the door to the lobby.

A uniformed footman appeared, almost as if he'd been part of the magic show. "I'm sorry, sir. Doors don't open until—"

Webb put his shield in front of the man's face. "Lieutenant Webb, NYPD. This is Detective O'Reilly. We're here to talk to Lucien."

"He's backstage, I think," the footman said, suddenly nervous. "But he's given specific instructions not to be disturbed."

"You don't need to point me to him, then," Webb said. "Just escort us backstage."

"Don't you need a warrant?"

"That would be true if we were searching for something," Webb said. "But this location isn't a crime scene... is it?"

The footman's face twitched. "Of course not! At least, I don't think so. Is it?" He looked suddenly very young.

"I've got no reason to think so," Webb said, giving him a slight smile. "So there's nothing to worry about."

"Okay," the man said doubtfully. "What about the dog?"

"NYPD K-9," Erin said. "What about him?"

The footman looked at her, then at the German Shepherd, and decided not to make an issue of it. "Okay," he said again. "This way."

He led them through an employee entrance and down a back hallway. They came out through another door into a space full of wooden crates and strange-looking pieces of equipment. Nobody else was in sight.

Webb and Erin stood there, looking around. Rolf looked at Erin for instructions. The footman made himself scarce, backing through the door they'd come from.

"Who disturbs the Amazing Lucien?" a deep bass voice boomed out. It sounded like it was coming from a shadowy corner. Erin saw a silhouette of a man there.

"Sir," Webb said, stepping toward the corner. "I'm Lieutenant Webb, NYPD. I just need to ask—"

"The Amazing Lucien demands that you look at him while addressing him!" the voice said sternly. Now it was coming from behind them. The silhouette slipped and caved in on itself like an empty bedsheet.

Erin spun around and reflexively dropped a hand to the grip of her Glock. Webb stopped dead in his tracks.

"Okay," Webb said. "You've had your fun. Are you ready to act like a grown-up now?"

"The Amazing Lucien will not be mocked!" the voice called. It had changed location again, and was behind them once more.

Erin was done with this. "Rolf, such," she said, giving the dog his "search" command. The Shepherd obediently put his nose to the concrete floor, snuffled a couple of times, and angled sharply left, Erin on his heels. He went around the back of a big crate and barked sharply, indicating he'd found someone.

Erin hurried after her dog and found herself face to face with a tall, good-looking man in a white button-down shirt and black slacks. He gave her a showman's grin with a mouthful of straight, white teeth.

"Okay, Detective," he said in a more normal voice, raising his hands theatrically. "You've got me. Red-handed." He twisted his right wrist and somehow, without Erin quite seeing how he did it, he was holding a red rose. He held it out to her, still smiling.

She didn't smile back. Cops didn't like it when people did unexpected things with their hands. "Cute trick," she said. "You'd be the Amazing Lucien?"

"Eager to astound and amaze you," he said, bowing slightly. "And well done. Illusions of the eye and ear are no match for such a discerning nose."

Webb caught up with Erin and glared at Lucien. "If you're done jerking us around, sir, we need to talk to you."

The magician continued smiling. "Of course. But remember, misdirection and deception are my stock in trade."

"I've heard of those," Erin said. "I think we call them obstruction of justice."

Webb sighed. "Let's start with your name. Your real name, please."

"It's true what they say," the magician said with a sigh of his own. "The police really do suck all the fun out of everything. I suppose if you were supposed to have a sense of humor, the department would have issued it to you with your badges and guns. But if that's the way you want it, here." He held out a plastic card in his left hand.

Erin blinked. She hadn't even seen his hand move.

Webb took the card and held it up, trying to catch the light of the overhead bulbs. Erin came forward and saw it was a Michigan state driver's license in the name Louis Miller.

"Thank you, Mr. Miller," Webb said. "Now, can you tell us the nature of your relationship with Kathy Grimes?"

"Kathy Grimes," Miller repeated. He stroked his chin with one hand. Then he snapped the fingers of his other hand. A flurry of sparks showered from his hand. "Yes, of course. She went by Kat. With a purr to match. And the claws, unfortunately."

"Were you romantically involved with her?" Webb asked.

"Romantically?" Miller laughed quietly. "No, I would hardly call it that."

"What would you call it?" Erin asked.

"A great many things," he said. "I suppose a dance of mutual attraction is the most appropriate description."

She resisted the urge to roll her eyes. "When's the last time you saw her?"

"Are you using the word in its literal or colloquial sense?"

"Literal."

He smiled again. "I suppose that question was irrelevant, because my previous answer remains unchanged. I saw her the night before last, sometime after midnight."

"Did she act unusual?" Webb asked.

"Not by her standards."

"What's that supposed to mean?" Erin asked.

"If your Lieutenant Webb, for example, were to exhibit similar behavior in my presence, I would find it unusual," Miller said. "I'm afraid I don't know you well enough to predict your actions, Detective."

"Do you know why anyone might want to harm her?" Webb asked.

"Ah," Miller said with an expression of sudden understanding. "You must be here about the unfortunate incident last night."

Webb gave him a slow, hard look. "You strike me as a fairly intelligent man, Mr. Miller," he said.

"Thank you, Lieutenant."

"What he means," Erin put in, "is that we recognize bullshit when we smell it, the same way my dog does."

"Then I hope never to have you on my stage as a volunteer," Miller said with that same flashy, showman's grin. "It seems you've caught me again. I did know why you were here. And yes, in the magicians' fraternity, we do keep a close eye on one another. I was aware of the accident, and I do understand that dear Kat, being unfortunately gifted with only one life rather than nine, is best spoken of in the nostalgic past tense."

"You don't seem very broken up about it," Erin said.

"I'm sure you've heard the phrase, 'the show must go on.'"

"Even when your girlfriend got sawed in half?"

"Your hearing is not on par with your sense of smell," Miller said. "As I said, the late Miss Grimes and I were not romantically entangled."

"Just physically," Webb said.

"Exactly," Miller said. "A not uncommon state of affairs. No pun intended, of course."

"So, just to be clear," Webb said. "You're not sorry she's dead?"

"If it were performed on stage," Miller said, "your leap of logic would require a safety net. I regret her demise, though I always thought the power saw stunt was needlessly dangerous. The safety protocols were slipshod. That was an accident waiting to happen."

"You sure it was an accident?" Erin asked.

Miller's smile was more genuine for a moment. "Detective O'Reilly," he said. "I've been a magician since I was sixteen. I can assure you, whatever happened on that stage, it was not what it appeared to be."

"Funny," she said. "Because it appeared a woman got cut in half with a buzzsaw. You saying that's not what happened?"

"I wasn't there," he said. "I'm only saying, there's more to this sort of thing than meets the eye."

*   *   *

"Is he our guy, O'Reilly?" Webb asked.

Erin stuck her hands in her pockets and suppressed a shiver. The January air whistled through the artificial canyons of Manhattan and stung her face. "I don't know," she said. "I'd like him to be."

Webb shook a cigarette out of its pack and lit up. "Goddamn Smoke Free Air Act," he muttered. "Can't smoke indoors in this crazy city. I'm gonna catch pneumonia and die."

"I think the law's intended to protect your lungs," she said.

"Ironic," he said. "But my lungs are a lost cause. The law's intended to protect yours."

"Miller's an asshole," she said. "But we can't arrest him for that."

"He's got motive," Webb said. "And he probably has the knowhow. He knows theater layout, and he just proved to us he can move around backstage. He's our best suspect so far. But you're right, we can't arrest him yet. We'd just end up turning him loose."

Erin sighed. "No kidding. We could hold him for forty-eight hours, put him in interrogation, see if he cracks."

"You think he'll crack?"

"Not likely."

"I don't either. Something wrong, O'Reilly?"

"What do you mean?"

"You keep looking around like you're expecting to get mugged."

"Just a little jumpy, sir."

Webb turned to look her in the eye. "How are you holding up, Detective?"

She looked straight back. "I'm fine, sir."

Chapter 6

The first thing Erin did when she got home at the end of her shift was to lock the door behind her. The second thing she did was pour herself a shot of whiskey. As the liquor burned down her throat into her stomach, she fed Rolf. Then she dropped onto the couch.

She felt empty and frustrated. The stupid, senseless waste of Kathy Grimes's death ate into her. People wanted to feel like their lives meant something. Their deaths, too. But cops knew better. Plenty of people lived pointless lives and died even more pointless deaths. But to die like that, chopped to pieces in front of a crowd of people, was worse than meaningless. It was obscene.

Erin couldn't tell whether the whiskey was making it easier or harder to think, so she got up and poured herself another. She stared at the amber liquid and reconstructed the crime scene in her memory. She saw the theater in her mind's eye, tried to remember the pattern of the blood, the way the body had been laid out. She remembered the stage props, the dungeon apparatus.

"Theater effects," she muttered.

Suddenly, she wished she hadn't taken that drink. She was right on the edge of figuring it out. It was right there, but she was too tired, too burned out. Other thoughts kept sneaking in, too, like a certain Irishman she'd been trying to put behind her. She put down her drink and rubbed her temples.

The knock on her door sent all her thoughts scampering for cover, like roaches in a kitchen when someone turned on the lights. Erin jumped to her feet. Rolf was up on his paws, too, staring at the door, ears perked.

Erin's apartment had a security door at the front. A visitor should've called up for her to buzz them in.

She drew her Glock and checked the chamber. Rolf picked up on her body language. His hackles rose. A low growl started deep in his chest.

Erin checked the peephole in the door. She was expecting some sort of trouble. But she wasn't expecting quite as much trouble as she saw.

Morton Carlyle stood in her hallway, alone. He was as neatly dressed as ever, in his customary charcoal suit and tie.

"What the hell do you want, Carlyle?" she called through the door.

"I'd like to speak with you, Erin. Preferably face to face."

She leaned against the door and tried to figure what to do. "Shit," she whispered. She glanced at the pistol in her hand. Carlyle's hands were empty. Besides, she wasn't scared of him. At least, not that way. She holstered the Glock. Then she took a deep breath and unlocked the door.

She opened it about halfway, making no move to step out of his way. Seeing his face, up close, brought a flood of memories, not all of them unwelcome. She saw the familiar look in his eye, remembered the hours of conversation, the secrets and dangers they'd faced together, their friendship. And she couldn't help remembering the feel of his skin, the scent of him, the taste of his lips.

Erin's jaw tightened. "Okay," she said. "Why are you here?"

He smiled slightly. "You told me to come."

"The hell I did."

"Perhaps Ian didn't recall your words correctly," he said. "But the lad's a fine scout. I hardly think he'd make an error on such a matter. You told him if I'd something to say, I knew where to find you."

"I blocked your goddamn phone," she growled. "Didn't that tell you anything?"

He nodded. "Aye, it told me you didn't trust yourself to talk to me."

"Why do you think that was?"

"Perhaps you'd some doubts about how things stood."

"Or maybe I didn't trust myself not to tear your damn head off. What the hell were you thinking?"

"I wasn't thinking, darling. Were you?"

"No! But you're always thinking, always playing an angle. What's the angle here, Carlyle? You like getting cozy with a detective?"

He wasn't smiling any longer. "If I'd thought my attentions unwelcome, I'd not have pressed them upon you."

"You've got a hit man stalking me!"

"Ian's no hit man, Erin," Carlyle said, and for the first time he showed a trace of anger. "He's a friend and a good lad. I trust him with my life."

"Why the hell was he following me?"

"I've been worried about you. You blocked my calls, you stopped coming to the Corner. I used to see you most days until our last encounter. Then you dropped off the Earth. I apologize if I hurt you. That was never my intention."

"So you expect me to believe he was protecting me?"

"That's what Ian does," Carlyle said. "He protects people."

"How long has he been shadowing me?"

"Only the past few days. I'd been wondering about you for a while, but I'd no wish to crowd you."

"How do you know him, anyway? He's got no record. He's a damn war hero. What's he got to do with you?"

"I'd be happy to explain, but perhaps we could do it more comfortably? It's hardly proper to talk across a doorway."

"Give me one good reason to let you in."

"If you truly wanted me gone, you'd have slammed the door in my face by now."

She very nearly did it. "Damn you, Carlyle. I'll give you ten minutes, tops."

*   *   *

"Would it be pressing my luck to ask for a drink?" he asked, glancing toward the kitchen.

"Get one back at the Corner," she shot back. "I'm almost out of whiskey."

"I've a bottle with your name on it."

"Want to know where you can stick that bottle? Clock's running. Start talking."

He walked into the living room. She followed him, suddenly and uncomfortably aware of the half-empty glass of whiskey on the coffee table. She was also aware that by choosing the ground, he was putting her on the defensive. Carlyle was a master negotiator for the Irish Mob, she reminded herself. He manipulated people for a living.

Rolf bristled at the Irishman and stuck close to Erin's side. Carlyle sat down at one end of her couch. She stayed standing.

"Erin, I scarce know where to begin," he said. "I should start with an apology, but I'm not regretting in the least what's passed between us. Save that it's driven a wedge. For that I'm truly sorry."

She didn't answer. She was watching his face, looking for anything he might give away.

"I've never meant you any harm," he went on. "I've considered you a friend for some time, and had hoped it might become something more."

"Even with you being what you are, and me what I am?" she replied.

"Aye, even then. A lad can hope."

She shook her head. "Christ. You're years older than I am. You're a damn terrorist and—"

"Retired," he interrupted gently.

"Retired terrorist," she corrected. "And gangster. You still middle management for Evan O'Malley?"

He nodded. "As you likely recall, when your lads hauled off Tommy Jay O'Malley for his part in the late unpleasantness with that German lad, it left a vacancy, which I now occupy."

"Great. You've been promoted. Congratulations." Erin put as much bitter sarcasm into her voice as she could. "I don't know what the hell I was thinking."

"I'd rather hoped you were thinking we'd worked well together, that we were good friends with a strong attraction."

"It'd been a rough day," she said. "I wasn't thinking straight. It just happened, you know?"

"Aye."

"And it was a mistake."

"If you think it was, I fear you're correct," Carlyle said. "But I'm here to make amends however I can. What can I do?"

"Is this a negotiation?"

He shook his head. "Think of it as a penance."

"Five Hail Marys and three Our Fathers? That sort of thing?"

A dry chuckle escaped him. "Maybe. What do you want from me, Erin?"

"If I wanted anything from you, I wouldn't have blocked your number."

"But I'm sitting here in your apartment. You must want something."

"Okay, how about some answers?"

"You've asked precious few questions as yet."

"Ian Thompson. Who is he?"

"A lad from Queens. His mum passed away when he was a wee lad, and his da was a worthless drunkard. The lad was running with street gangs when I met him, a hard lad at the ripe age of twelve. I could see he was heading from trouble to worse. I took an interest in steering him a straighter path."

"I don't believe this," she said. "You telling me you mentored him?"

"You could call it that. I got him off the streets and back into school, helped him to his high school diploma."

"So he'd come work for you?"

"I didn't want that for him," Carlyle said. "Besides, he'd a desire to join the military. The lad had something to prove to himself. So he went overseas, and I fear more trouble found him. He came back changed."

"How so?" Erin asked, thinking of the medal citation she'd seen.

"He was more polite, but colder." Carlyle shrugged. "He'd been in battle, seen and done dreadful things. He doesn't like to talk about it. The lad was lacking direction, but was in possession of a particular set of skills, so I took him on as a bodyguard and driver. You've my word, he does nothing illegal."

"So why's he following me? It's not just because you're worried I didn't return your phone calls."

Carlyle nodded. "Tommy Jay's absence has been noted by my colleagues. While the lad was a right bastard, if you'll pardon my saying it, the way he was removed was a trifle unusual."

"Guys in the life get busted all the time," she pointed out.

"Aye, but this lad was taken down by a lass I'd a connection with. As I then took his place, it's got some of the lads wondering what exactly the nature of our relationship might be."

"Great," Erin said. "Just great. So the O'Malleys know? Did you tell them all the juicy details?"

"I've told no one," Carlyle answered. "I told Evan that you and I exchanged information unrelated to the O'Malleys, in order to remove his competition and take care of particular problems. Though I fear Corky may have tumbled to something, on account of your abrupt absence from the Corner."

She sighed. James Corcoran, Carlyle's best friend, was exactly the sort of man who'd figure out that sort of thing. He'd tried to sleep with Erin once, almost succeeded, and remained a shameless flirt. "So, what are you telling me? Are mob guys gonna try to whack me? That's why Ian's on my ass?"

"It's merely a precaution," he said. "Until everyone gets used to the new chain of command. The lad won't bother you, I promise."

"And if I tell you to send him somewhere else?"

Carlyle shrugged. "That's your choice."

"Your ten minutes are just about up," she said. "Anything you're desperate to tell me, before I throw you out?"

He stood and looked her square in the eye. "My wife was murdered almost twenty years ago," he said quietly. "Since that day, the only time I've felt anything close to what I did with her is when I've been with you. I understand it's a complicated situation, but if you think I'll let you pull away from me without putting up the best fight of which an Irishman's capable, you're mistaken. I'll be on my way tonight, Erin, but I'll be coming back to you. I promise."

Erin was still trying to work out her reply as he went out the door. Rolf watched him go, then turned his eyes on her and nudged her with his snout. She absently dropped a hand and scratched him between the ears.

"Good boy," she murmured. At least there was one guy in her life she understood.

Chapter 7

"Congratulations," Webb said. He tossed the day's issue of the New York Times onto each detective's desk. Erin, still bleary from a restless night, squinted at the paper and tried to make sense of the headlines.

"We're front-page news," the Lieutenant continued. "I've just gotten off the phone with Captain Holliday. He likes being above the fold, but only when we close a case. Last time we made page one, it was that thing at the Civic Center. We won that round. Does this feel like victory to you?"

Erin focused. "Bloodbath in Manhattan," she read aloud. "Police search for answers in brutal theater slaying."

"Nice," Vic growled. "Time for our pep talk, boss?"

"I haven't got any pep," Webb said. "What I've got is one of the most public murders in the history of New York City. I want answers, people."

"What's the word on getting another detective?" Vic asked. "To replace Kira."

"I'm sorry," Webb said. "I didn't realize the workload was too much for you. I'll get right on that."

"Someone woke up on the wrong side of his life this morning," Vic muttered.

"What's that, Neshenko?"

"Sorry," Vic said. "I should've said someone woke up on the wrong side of his life this morning, sir."

"That's better. The first thing I want is a closer look at Miss Grimes. We know about Louis Miller. Let's find out if she had any other boyfriends or affairs. Check her financials for anything shady. She's got a record. She may have made enemies somewhere along the way. O'Reilly, look into that grand larceny charge from Detroit."

"Sir, that was years ago," she said.

"I know, but she walked. It's a possible motive. See what you can dig up. Neshenko, you're on the money trail."

Vic sighed loudly and turned to his computer. Erin got herself a fresh cup of coffee from the department's espresso machine and got ready for some boring data mining.

* * *

"That's funny," Erin said.

"I could use a laugh," Vic said.

"The manager Grimes was accused of ripping off," she said. "Hugo Bucklington."

"Okay, the name's a little funny," he agreed.

"That's not what I meant. He's here, in New York."

That got Vic and Webb's attention. "He's not in Detroit?" Webb asked.

"Court documents from Michigan," she explained. "Bucklington's contact info got updated three months ago. He's living in the Bronx."

"That's something," Webb said. "You've got an address?"

"And phone number and employer," she confirmed.

"Let's go get him," Vic said, jumping to his feet.

"Sit down, Neshenko," Webb said. "I'm still waiting for your report on her financials. O'Reilly and I will take care of Bucklington."

"Damn." Vic sat back down with a scowl.

"Where's he work?" Webb asked Erin as they headed for the door. Vic glared at them.

"Auto body repair," she said. "Crash Course Collision."

"Let's give him a little surprise," he said. "If we rattle him enough, maybe we can get a confession, wrap this up by lunchtime."

They took Erin's car, since it had a compartment for Rolf. Webb spent the drive reading up on the old Larceny case. They found Crash Course Collision in a "recovering neighborhood." That was the term used by the same people who called Third World warzones "developing countries." The best thing that could be said was that no one shot at them as they parked. The shop was a broken-down brick building with a scrapyard next door. The yard was surrounded by a chain-link fence, topped by razor wire and populated by the corpses of wrecked automobiles.

"Better lock your doors," Webb observed. "I guess I know why he left Detroit. He is definitely on the skids."

"This must remind him of home," Erin said.

They hadn't even gotten halfway to the front door when a huge, black, furry thing hurled itself against the fence. It didn't look like any animal Erin had ever seen, but judging from the ferocious barking, she knew it had to be some kind of dog. It snarled and sprayed saliva through the chain links at them. Rolf went stiff-legged and bristling, growling low in his throat.

"Steady, boy," Erin said quietly. "Fuss."

That was his "heel" command. Rolf stuck obediently at her side, but his hackles stayed up.

Webb went in first, pushing through a door painted an ugly, peeling green. It opened on a dingy little office with a young guy sitting behind a counter watching TV. He glanced up, saw the three of them, and did a double take.

"Shit, man," he said. "You can't bring that dog in here. Ripper gonna kill him!"

Erin pointed a thumb to the window, where the black beast was apparently trying to dig through the glass to get at them. "That's Ripper?"

"Hell, yes. He a killin' machine!"

"And this is an NYPD K-9," Erin said. "So I think it's in all our best interests to keep them apart."

"Hey, it's cool," the kid said. He gave Erin a long, appreciative look. "You cops? Damn, you the finest cop I seen outside the movies."

"I get that a lot," Webb deadpanned. "You have a Hugo Bucklington working here?"

"Hell, yes. He in back, workin' on a '87 Aries. Talk about your shitmobiles, man. Weary old K-car. I tell him you here." He went to the back door and opened it a few inches. The sound of some sort of power tool got suddenly much louder.

"Hey, Hugo!" the kid shouted at the top of his lungs. "Five-O here for you, man!"

"Damn," Webb said quietly. "Should've seen that coming."

The sound of the machine suddenly stopped. A metal tool clattered on concrete. Then they heard running footsteps, headed away from them.

"Go," Webb said to Erin.

Normally she'd have turned Rolf loose in pursuit, but she didn't fancy getting him mixed up with Ripper. Erin started running, Rolf loping easily alongside. The kid thought it was funny until Webb grabbed him. The last she saw of them as she raced into the garage was the Lieutenant flipping the boy around and putting him face-first against the wall.

The garage was full of half-assembled autos, a maze of old Detroit steel. Rolf was straining at his leash, knowing they were in the chase. She followed his lead but kept her grip on him. He led her through the garage to a small back door which stood a little ajar. Then they were through it and into the scrapyard.

As she went, she drew her Glock. Erin loved dogs. If Ripper went for her, or for Rolf, she could legally shoot the animal. But she didn't want to, no matter how vicious a bastard the junkyard dog might be.

Ripper wasn't about to make the decision easy. He came around an Oldsmobile station wagon, all black fur, white teeth, and beady, murderous eyes. Erin had a frozen split second when she wished she had her Patrol gear, especially her Taser. Rolf tensed himself for a fight.

"Down!" Erin shouted, putting all her dog-trainer's authority into the word. Never show fear, they'd taught her. Never doubt that the dog will do what you want. You don't ask them to do something. You tell them what they're going to do, and you already know they will.

Ripper skidded to a stop. He stared at the woman and the other dog. Then, obediently, he sank to his haunches. He flattened onto his belly. His ears drooped and he whined a little. Something scraggly that might have been his tail wagged ingratiatingly.

"Stay," she ordered. "Good boy." While she spoke, she was looking around the yard for Bucklington. She saw movement at the far corner of the lot. Hugo appeared to be trying to climb the fence by means of the cab of a Ford pickup.

Ripper had a metal-studded collar. Erin took hold of it, firmly but not cruelly. The dog cringed as she did it. She flinched inwardly, knowing this dog had been beaten into submission.

"Rolf," she said, unsnapping his lead with her other hand, "such."

Rolf sprang into motion. He covered the length of the scrapyard in a matter of seconds. Before Hugo Bucklington had managed to clamber to the top of the fence, the Shepherd was barking and scrambling up onto the hood of the Ford.

"Give it up!" Erin shouted at him. "He wants to bite you. Come on down, or I'll let him!"

Bucklington cautiously descended, keeping as far from the K-9 as he could. Erin reflected that people who beat animals had a tendency to be afraid of them.

"Hands where I can see them!" she ordered. Improvising, she clipped Rolf's leash to Ripper's collar and quickly tied the junkyard dog to the doorframe of a car with busted-out windows. Then she advanced on Bucklington. "Turn around! Hands behind your head!"

He kept looking nervously at Rolf. Rolf wasn't about to put him at ease. The Shepherd kept growling, waiting for Erin's "bite" command. His tail was sweeping from side to side with eager excitement.

Erin took advantage of the distraction to close the distance, keeping her Glock on him. Hugo Bucklington was a big guy, but with more fat than muscle. She got the cuffs on him and frisked him for weapons, finding none.

"Hugo Bucklington?" she asked.

"What?"

"You're gonna need to come with us, answer some questions."

"I didn't do anything!"

He was facing away from her, so couldn't see her roll her eyes. "Says the guy who ran the second the cops showed up," she said. "C'mon, let's go."

*   *   *

Webb had the kid in custody by the time Erin got back inside. He gave Erin a thin smile. "Good catch. Let's get them back to the precinct."

"You takin' us to the Five Four?" the kid asked.

"How old are you, anyway?" Webb asked in reply.

"Why you wanna know?"

"Because you look like you're about fourteen," the Lieutenant said. "And for a kid that age, you know way too much about the NYPD. No, we're not going to the Fifty-Fourth. We're taking you to Manhattan, Precinct 8."

"You guys with ACIS?" the kid asked, naming the Auto Crime Division.

"We're with Major Crimes," Webb said. "But now that you mention it, I'm sure ACIS will be interested to have a talk with you, once we're through."

"It's gonna be a tight squeeze in the Charger," Erin said, thinking of Rolf's compartment. It took up half the back seat.

"They can get cozy," Webb said.

"What about Ripper?" she asked.

"Huh?"

"The junkyard dog," she said. "If we're busting these two mopes, I'm not gonna just leave him out there for God knows how long."

Erin looked at Bucklington and Devon. "Which one of you owns that dog?"

Bucklington didn't say anything.

"He belong to himself, mostly," Devon said. "But I feed him, sometimes."

"And hit him to make him behave," she added.

"You seen him. He crazy!"

"You have someone you can call, to come look after him?"

"I guess."

"Then you can ring him up from the precinct."

Once they got the prisoners and Rolf loaded into the squad car, Erin went back for Rolf's leash. Ripper growled when she approached and crouched, ready for trouble.

"Sit," she said.

Ripper sat.

"Down."

Down he went.

"Good boy." She unfastened the leash and stepped back, still facing him, making him see she was boss. "You just stay here."

The black, shaggy beast watched her go. She thought she saw a hint of a wag in his tail.

Chapter 8

The kid was Devon James, age sixteen. Given the short time span of his criminal career, he'd built a pretty impressive rap sheet. Mostly juvenile stuff, but he'd lately graduated to Grand Theft Auto. He was actually supposed to be in Juvenile Detention, from what Erin could see, but someone somewhere had screwed up and he was back on the street. For the moment.

"Looks like they're running a chop shop," Vic observed over Erin's shoulder. They were back at the precinct, checking up on their suspects before starting the interrogation.

"Probably," she agreed. "The crummy old cars I saw there were cover. I expect they move the real merchandise through as fast as they can."

"I thought this guy worked for General Motors," Vic said.

"He did," Webb said. "I just checked with GM. He got laid off a month after Grimes's trial. He'd started with their maintenance division before he made manager, so he already had the skill set to slot into a nice life of crime."

"Think he got canned because of the mess with Grimes?" Vic wondered.

"It's a possibility." Webb stood up. "I think we've got enough to go on. O'Reilly, you're with me."

"This should be good," Vic muttered. "I guess I'll watch on the sideline. Like usual."

*   *   *

The usual rule of thumb with interrogations, when there were multiple suspects, was to start with the weakest one and work your way up. Normally this would mean starting with the teenager. Since he was 16, James was old enough to be interviewed without parental consent. But Webb went to Bucklington's interrogation room first.

"The kid's a hard case," he explained, one hand on the door. "Practically born in the life."

"Bucklington doesn't have a record," Erin agreed. "He'll crack easier, you think?"

"He hasn't lawyered up yet," Webb said. "So he's either inexperienced or an idiot. Either way, we'll take him apart." He opened the door.

Hugo Bucklington was cuffed to the table inside. He looked scared, but also a little confused, like he'd been hit on the head. He looked from one detective to the other and smiled hesitantly. Erin had to admit, he looked soft. She'd been around a lot of criminals and was used to their defense mechanisms. Bucklington didn't have any. He looked like a random blue-collar guy, like the neighbors she'd had growing up in Queens. Pudgy, middle-aged, balding. The sort of guy you'd call if your plumbing clogged up.

On the other hand, murderers could look harmless. It didn't pay to make assumptions.

"You're a long way from Detroit, Mr. Bucklington," Webb said, taking a seat opposite him.

"Detroit?" the prisoner repeated.

"Motor City," Webb said. "Motown. Detroit."

"Oh. Yeah. That's where I'm from. Say, could you or the lady tell me what's going on here?"

"We just need you to answer some questions for us," Webb said. "Can you tell me where you were on New Year's Eve?"

"I was at home. Well, not Detroit, that is. I have an apartment in the Bronx."

"All day?" Erin asked.

"Huh? No, just for the evening. I was working during the day."

"Who can vouch for your whereabouts?"

"Devon. He was at the shop all day." Bucklington's face fell. "But you arrested him, too, so maybe you won't believe that."

"We'll see," Webb said. "You're pretty handy with machinery, aren't you?"

"Yeah, I guess."

"You go to school for that?"

"Henry Ford Community College. Automotive Technology." A little pride showed in his voice.

"You had a pretty good thing going with GM."

"Yeah. While it lasted."

"How'd you lose the job?"

"The economy. Lots of guys got canned."

"What'd Kathy Grimes have to do with it?"

"What?" Bucklington asked.

"Kathy Grimes," Webb said patiently. "Tell me about her."

"That bitch?" For the first time, an expression other than bewilderment and fear was on Bucklington's face. "She played me. She got in close, all cozy-like, made me think we had something special. Then she ripped me off. Cleaned out the department petty cash account, using my access."

"Did she use your work computer?" Webb asked.

"Remote access, from home," Bucklington said more quietly.

"Were you having an affair with Miss Grimes?" Erin asked.

He snorted. "I was having an affair," he said bitterly. "She was playing games with me."

"How did she get away with it?" Webb asked. "She was acquitted at trial."

Bucklington snorted again. "Reasonable doubt. They couldn't find the money anywhere. Her lawyer said it could've just as easily been me. My word against hers. I hope that lawyer was expensive. She sure got her money's worth from him. Hell, maybe she was screwing him, too. Wouldn't surprise me."

"What happened afterward?" Webb asked.

"GM sacked me three days after the trial," he answered unhappily. "By that time my wife had already moved out. They said it was the economy, but the truth is, they just didn't trust me anymore. Word got around, and I couldn't get another job in Detroit. So I headed out east to try my luck."

"Where you ran into Kathy again," Webb said.

"What're you talking about? Kathy's still in Detroit," Bucklington said. "Far as I know."

"No, she was in Manhattan on New Year's Eve," Webb prompted. "What do you think she was doing?"

"Screwing some poor bastard over," Bucklington said. "That's what she does. Look, Detective, I don't know what's going on here, but if it's anything to do with Kathy Grimes, it's nothing to do with me. She and I are done. Over. I'm not working with her!"

"I didn't say you were," Webb said softly. "You really hate her, don't you?"

"She took my job, my money, and my marriage, okay? Of course I hate her!"

Webb nodded sympathetically. "I can see why. She pretty much ruined your life."

"You're damned right she did!"

"You ever think about getting even with her?"

"I used to dream about it," Bucklington said. He sat back and stared into space, remembering. "She's got this great, sparkly smile, like you see in a toothpaste commercial. I dreamed about taking a tire iron to those pretty white teeth of hers."

Erin winced inwardly. That was not a wise thing to say in an interrogation room.

"You'd like her to be dead, wouldn't you?" Webb suggested, soft and encouraging.

"The day I hear she's dead," Bucklington said, looking Webb straight in the eye, "I'll get a case of beer, drink about six cans, then go to the cemetery and piss it all out on her grave."

"Then this is your lucky day," Webb said with a smile. "Tell you what. Why don't you tell me how you did it, and maybe we can get you that beer you're wanting."

"Huh?" Confusion and fear crowded the anger back out of Bucklington's face. "Did what?"

"Kathy," Webb said patiently. "Tell me how you killed her. You already told us why."

"Kathy's dead?"

Erin and Webb nodded in unison.

"Wait, you think I killed her?" he exclaimed.

The detectives waited and watched him.

"No! I didn't! I would never!"

"Take a tire iron to those pretty white teeth?" Erin repeated.

"I was just saying that! I didn't mean it!"

"You meant it a minute ago," Erin said, stepping into the role of bad cop. "She was killed brutally. Painfully. By someone who really hated her. Someone like you, Mr. Bucklington. Listen, this is a bad situation. You're lucky they don't put people in the electric chair anymore in the great state of New York. But once they hang this around your neck, you're never getting out of prison. The inmates, they've got special plans for guys who kill girls. Maybe, just maybe, if you can explain this, tell us how you did it, come clean, you might get a shot at parole before you die behind bars."

Bucklington looked wildly from Webb's face to Erin's, a trapped animal looking for a way out. "No, you have to believe me! I wanted to hurt her, sure, but I didn't! I didn't even know she was in New York, I swear to God!"

"How did you get backstage at the theater?" Webb pressed on relentlessly. "Help me so I can help you."

"What theater? I wasn't at any theater! I was working New Year's Eve!"

"Can you prove it?" Erin challenged.

Bucklington froze for a few seconds in sheer, blind panic. Then his face lit up. "Yeah! Yeah, I can! I sold a bunch of parts off a Mercedes to a guy."

"A Mercedes?" Erin repeated. "You expect us to believe that? You were working on a piece of shit from the '80s when we rolled up on you. You don't get high-end crap like that. If you're gonna feed me bullshit, make it something believable."

"No, it was a Mercedes," Bucklington said. "I swear. I can give you the guy. His name's Ed Kane. He deals parts to street racers and local garages, behind the scenes."

"When did you meet with this Mr. Kane?" Webb asked.

"Four o'clock, more or less." He looked hopeful. "Was that around the time Kathy died?"

"And your dealings with Mr. Kane would be illegal?" Webb prompted.

"Well, yeah, technically."

"And this Mercedes was stolen?"

"I don't know. I didn't ask."

"But you didn't receive the vehicle title."

"No."

"So, your alibi is that you were receiving stolen merchandise."

Bucklington hesitated, then nodded. "Yeah."

"We're going to need a detailed statement about this," Webb said. "Everything you did on the 31st, start to finish. Who you talked to, who you met with, how much money changed hands. Everything."

* * *

Vic gave them a slow round of applause as they left the interrogation room. "That was beautiful, boss. Absolutely beautiful. You said you were gonna get a confession, and you did. I mean, it was a confession to a totally different crime, but still..."

"Can it, Neshenko," Webb said. Then a smile crossed his face, almost against his will. "Okay, I admit it. That was a good one."

"We need to check the whole thing out," Erin said. "Those guys are all gonna lie about it. It's the worst alibi in the world."

"Yeah," Webb said. "But we'll be able to kick some of the legwork over to Auto Crimes, at least. And in the meantime, let's find out who else wanted Kathy Grimes dead."

"I'm starting to get the feeling it's gonna be a long list," Vic said.

Chapter 9

"This is hopeless," Vic said.

For once, Webb didn't comment on Vic's pessimism. The three detectives stared morosely at a map of the United States. Webb had stuck it to their whiteboard. Erin and Vic had plotted the Great Ronaldo's tour of the lower forty-eight with a red Sharpie. It made a meandering trail of crimson that hit Detroit, Chicago, Cleveland, Philadelphia, and Boston before coming to a stop in New York.

"We can't check six major cities for tangential crimes," Webb said. "It'll be the damn phone book." He twirled an unlit cigarette in his fingers.

"It was just a theory, anyway," Erin said. It had been her idea that Kathy Grimes might have been using her role with the magic show as a cover for larceny.

"But it makes sense," Webb said. "Sideshow performers have a tendency to engage in that kind of behavior."

"I wish Kira was here," Vic said. "She'd have some fun fact for us, like how getting 'gypped' is an old ethnic slur on Gypsies."

"Sounds like we don't need her," Webb said. "You're a fountain of knowledge."

"Only about persecuted ethnic groups from eastern Europe," he replied.

"Anyway," Webb said, "it's unlikely any local victim would've followed her to New York. They wouldn't have had much time to plan, and the chances they were familiar enough with stage equipment... It's thin."

"We letting Bucklington go?" Erin asked.

"Yeah," Webb said. "He'll go all the way to the Fifty-Fourth. They'll take him in for the car theft he's confessed to. If we need him again, they'll have him in a nice, cozy cell. After that, he'll be in Riker's if he can't make bail."

"And I don't think he's exactly rolling in money," Vic added. "How about Whitaker?"

"He's not going anywhere, either," Webb said. "If he leaves town, I've told him he'll be trying to outrun a warrant. If he crosses state lines, it'll be the Marshals on his ass."

"I'd like to see him pull a disappearing act on them," Vic chuckled.

"Last I heard, he was looking for a new assistant," Webb continued.

"Who's gonna be crazy enough to take that job?" Erin wondered aloud.

"With this publicity and exposure?" Vic retorted. "There'll be wannabe celebrities lined up around the block. Ten bucks says so."

"No bet," Erin said. Carlyle, professional bookie, would've agreed it was a sucker's wager.

"We need more," Webb said softly, tapping his cigarette against his upper lip thoughtfully.

"Maybe someone should talk to Whitaker again, or Miller," Erin said.

"You want to?" Webb asked.

"Hell no," she said. "These guys give me the creeps. But I think it's a good idea. I want to understand how their world works a little better. Who they come in contact with, how they do their business. I understand drug rings, mob families, street gangs, sure. But magicians are different."

Webb nodded. "Okay. Why don't you talk to Miller? These stage types are pretty close-mouthed about their own tricks. He may open up a little more about his competitor."

Erin's dad had told her something similar about busting street gangs. "No one wants to rat out his buddies. But they can rationalize squealing on a rival. They'll even insist they're not a rat afterwards."

"I'll head over now," she said. "I should be able to catch him before he starts prepping for the evening show."

"He's staying at the Hilton Times Square," Vic said. "But if he invites you in, watch his hands. If he grabs your ass, shoot him."

* * *

Erin pulled out of the Precinct 8 parking garage in her Charger, Rolf riding in his compartment in back. She checked the rearview mirror to see if she was being followed. The black Lincoln Town Car in her lane was a little suspicious. Two guys were riding in it, and the windows looked to be tinted right on the edge of the legal limit. She told herself she was being silly, turned north on 8th Avenue, and checked the mirror again.

The car was still there.

She went a couple of blocks, waiting for it to turn or change lanes. It didn't.

Who were those guys? She thought of Ian Thompson, but Ian was apparently a lone operator, and there were two men in the car. Other mob associates, maybe, like Carlyle was worried about.

That was assuming Carlyle was telling the truth. Erin wondered about that. He was cagey, sure, but he was also very good at never actually lying to her. Everything he'd ever said that she'd been able to check had turned out to be true, technically.

She turned southeast on 34th. It was out of her way, but that was part of the test. If they stuck with her through her zigzag, she could be pretty sure they were tailing her. She went north again on 6th Avenue.

The Town Car stuck with her.

Erin maintained her speed. She didn't want to spook her tail. But she kept an increasingly sharp eye on them and eased a hand to the Glock at her belt. If it was a hit, they'd wait for her to come to a red light and pull up alongside. If she saw them coming up on her with windows down, she'd know for sure. Then she'd have about five seconds to figure out how to stay alive.

She got to 40th Street without incident and turned right, starting a circuit around Bryant Park and the New York Public Library. Her plan was to circle the library at 5th Avenue and hook back up 42nd Street to the Hilton. There was no way the other car would follow her by accident.

Sure enough, the Town Car followed her onto 40th. The light at 5th Avenue was red as she approached in the left-hand lane, with two cars stopped in front of her. The other car moved into the next lane over. It edged forward.

Its windows were still rolled up, but Erin wasn't taking any chances. She flicked her remote stoplight control. Every police car had one these days, enabling them to change lights as they approached. It messed with traffic flow and pissed off city engineers, but it could make all the difference in response time. The light obligingly turned green.

Erin quickly went left. The Town Car blinked its turn signal, but another car had pulled up behind her and they couldn't find a space. The driver had no choice but to continue straight across 5th Avenue and away from her. Erin, looking in her rearview as she accelerated away from them, was sure the driver was watching her. She caught a glimpse of a square-faced guy wearing a watch cap; not enough to pull out of a lineup.

Another car was right behind the Lincoln, a nondescript off-white Toyota, and for an instant, Erin thought she caught a glimpse of a familiar buzz-cut silhouette behind its wheel. Now that looked like Ian Thompson.

She shrugged the thought away. Whatever had happened, or nearly happened, she'd dodged it. It didn't scare her; it pissed her off. Erin expected perps to run away, not trail after her. She'd have to take care of this, one way or another. But in the meantime, she still had a job to do.

*   *   *

The clerk at the Hilton was surly and unhelpful until Erin showed her shield. Then he became surly but cooperative. As far as he knew, Louis Miller was still in the building, in his suite on the forty-fourth floor. "It's fine to bring your pet in," he added, "but you can't leave him unattended."

"I don't see any pets here," Erin retorted and led her dog to the elevators.

She was glad it was January Second, and not the First. Times Square wasn't a cop's favorite place to be on New Year's. Bits of confetti nestled in the corners of the elevator, waiting for the overworked custodial staff to finish cleaning up after the biggest party of the year. As she waited for the elevator to reach the appointed floor, she leaned against the wall and pressed the bridge of her nose with her fingers. So far, the year was turning out to be one long hangover.

Maybe the Lincoln hadn't been following her. And that guy in the second car had only been visible for a second. He might've been some random New Yorker who looked a little like Ian Thompson. Besides, the Irish Mob wasn't about to whack a police detective in the middle of Manhattan in broad daylight. That would be insane.

She tried to concentrate on the job at hand. Miller was a slippery son of a bitch, and she'd need to be on her A-game to keep up with him. She organized her thoughts as best she could, squared her shoulders, and watched the numbers on the elevator.

Erin knocked on the door to the King Deluxe Suite, wondering for a moment what it would cost to spend a night there. Hundreds of dollars, naturally. Everything in Manhattan cost hundreds of dollars.

After a short pause, the door swung open to reveal Louis Miller in an honest-to-God crimson silk bathrobe. He'd obviously just stepped out of the shower. Erin saw a thin haze of steam in the air, and his hair was still wet. He gave her his best showman's smile, all straight white teeth and dark, intense eyes.

"What a surprise," he said. "If it isn't Detective... O'Reilly, unless I'm mistaken. And woman's best friend at her side. I can only imagine what brings you to my door. Come in, please, and do forgive my... ah, disheveled state. I wasn't expecting company."

"I thought magicians could see the future," she said, stepping inside and reflexively checking the corners of the room. No one else was there. The living room was well furnished, with panoramic windows offering a great view of Times Square. Far below, a few workmen still scurried around, sweeping up the remains of New Year's Eve while the business of the city went on around them.

"Perhaps I can," Miller laughed. "But I don't think I should tell you your future."

"Why's that?" she asked, moving to the bedroom doorway and making sure that room was empty, too.

"You seem the sort who would do the opposite of what I said, simply to prove me wrong," he said, still smiling.

"You told me you were sixteen when you took up magic," she said. "Why'd you start?"

"I wished to unlock the secrets of the mystical universe and initiate myself into its underlying truth."

She lifted an eyebrow.

His smile became more self-deprecating. "Well, that, and I wanted to impress a girl in study hall."

That got an answering smile from her. "What tricks did you learn?"

"Oh, all sorts," he said. "I bought a book of sleight-of-hand. You know, making coins pop out of ears, pulling scarves out of sleeves, that sort of thing. Simple tricks, not needing much in the way of props."

"Did they work?"

"Oh yes, definitely." Miller's eyes took on a dreamy cast, remembering. "Mindy Cartwright," he said. "I took her to the Homecoming Dance in eleventh grade. That night I learned there were all kinds of magic, and I'd only scratched the surface."

"Want to show me a trick?"

"Would it impress you?"

"Try me."

Miller nodded and held up a finger on his left hand. "I'd be delighted. But just a moment. You've caught me a little unprepared. Let's see…" He made an exaggerated show of patting the pockets of his robe. "Ah, here we are!" He snapped the fingers of his right hand. A cigar appeared between his index and middle fingers. He held it out toward her.

"I don't smoke," Erin said. "And it's not allowed here."

"Hmm, you're right," Miller said. He raised it to his lips. "But maybe just a puff. If I have a light..." A gold cigarette lighter appeared in his other hand. He flicked it, but instead of a flame, a small cloud of multicolored sparks popped and fizzled out the top. Erin blinked, and saw the cigar had been replaced by a carrot.

"Much healthier, you'd agree," he said, spinning it around in his hand and offering it to her.

"You're quick," she said, looking at the carrot. It was, indeed, a carrot.

"Not particularly," he said. "Speed isn't the point. The point is misdirection."

"I was watching the wrong hand," she said, understanding.

He grinned. "The point of every magic trick is for the audience to be watching the wrong thing. However, this is crucial, they need to think they're watching the right thing. People have to imagine they've seen something miraculous, not simply missed the moment. It's all smooth showmanship, Detective. I suppose it's the exact opposite of what you do."

"And what's that?"

"You seek to dispel deception. I encourage it. You want answers. I enjoy making people ask questions. Would you like something to drink?"

"Thanks, but I'm on duty."

"Very well," he said. "If you don't mind, I'll just fix one for myself." He went to the minibar and deftly mixed himself a cocktail, using ingredients from the bar and a few things from a brown paper bag on the table. He came up with a drink that was a very unusual color, a sort of sparkly black.

"What's that?" she couldn't help asking.

"Black magic," he said with a smile. "You want to try one?"

"What's in it?"

"I can't tell you. Trade secret."

"In that case, no thanks."

He settled himself into an armchair and sipped his drink. "You want to ask questions, I want you to ask them."

"I want you to answer them," she corrected.

His smile showed just a hint of teeth between his lips. "Maybe we'll both get what we want."

"What do you think of Ron Whitaker?"

"The Great Ronaldo? He's a good technical magician, but he trusts his toys a little too much."

"How do you mean?"

"He relies on gadgets more than on stagecraft and showmanship. He lacks flair and substitutes for it with dangerous stunts. It really was only a matter of time before some awful mishap occurred."

"Have you known him long?"

"We stage magicians are a small community. Even more so in Detroit. Michigan isn't exactly known for masters of the arcane arts. Ron and I have known of each other most of our careers."

"Would you call him a rival?"

"Everyone on Earth is a rival for something. Food, shelter, fame, power, women..."

"Which one of you is the better magician?"

Miller's smile widened. "You get right to the heart of the matter," he said. "Surely you don't think I did away with the Great Ronaldo's assistant out of some misplaced sense of jealousy, do you?"

"Did you?"

Miller's eyes were unreadable. "If I did, I certainly wouldn't simply come out and say so."

He reminded her very much of a mobster in that moment. It was exactly the same sort of answer Carlyle would have given. Magicians liked mystery. They liked playing the game. But this wasn't a game. A woman had died.

"What did Kathy Grimes want from you?" she asked, deliberately shifting gears.

He didn't even blink. "Quite a few things."

"Such as?"

"She'd heard some things about me," he said, looking her lazily up and down. "She wanted to know if they were true."

"Besides the sex," Erin said, not letting him get to her.

"Something you should understand about Kat," Miller said. "She was a manipulator, particularly of men. Everything she did was for her own advancement. It was always a bargain, a deal, or a scam. But it was never enough just to put one over on an unsuspecting fellow. She was a con artist who was like a graffiti tagger. She couldn't resist whenever she saw a nice patch of wall. She always had to paint her name. That's what made her such a good stage assistant. She loved the spotlight. I think she always wanted to be one of those reality-TV starlets. You might shudder at the thought of your private life splashed across the pages of the tabloids. She thrilled at it."

"So what was Kathy's con? What was her angle on you?"

"She wanted to learn my trade secrets."

"So she could take them to Whitaker?"

Miller looked thoughtful. "I think she wanted to be a magician in her own right," he said. "Or perhaps just an accomplished pickpocket. The skill sets are virtually interchangeable."

"Did she steal anything from you?"

"Nothing I was sorry to see her take."

"Did you take anything from her?"

"Besides the obvious?" He didn't quite wink, but managed to imply it.

"Yeah, besides that." She didn't smile.

"She offered an exchange."

"Of what?" Erin paused. "Besides the obvious," she added.

"Secrets."

"Magic tricks?"

He nodded.

"Did you agree?"

"I showed her some things," he said. "Simple sleights-of-hand that she could sex up with her stage presence. Nothing terribly valuable."

"Did you like her?"

The sudden change of tack startled Miller, but he was quick to recover his poise. Erin was sure he'd had plenty of practice on stage when things went wrong. "I did, if you believe it. Kat was easy to like, in spite of her flaws. It was only after she left on each visit that I recalled the ways she could be difficult and irritating. She had charisma. I swear, the woman could explain away a bloody butcher's knife in her hand and a body at her feet, and do it so convincingly you'd never question it until you were halfway home."

"Maybe that's why she was killed the way she was," Erin said out loud.

"A booby trap would prevent the killer from hesitating," Miller agreed. "Or from having second thoughts." His smile took on a hint of sadness. "It's a pity Kat couldn't fully appreciate the manner of her death. The theatricality of it would have pleased her."

"I don't think that was on her mind while it was happening," Erin said sourly. "Thanks for your time, Mr. Miller. If you think of anything else, please give me a call."

"What if all I'm looking for is some light dinner conversation with a charming woman?"

"Then you better call someone else."

Chapter 10

Erin ended the day tired, grumpy, and with a headache. They'd gotten no closer to finding Kathy Grimes's killer. In fact, what she'd learned had left Erin with a certain amount of sympathy for the evil bastard who'd murdered her. Kathy didn't seem to have had a single genuine friend in the world. There were just people she played off each other to get what she wanted.

They'd spent the rest of the day tracking Ronaldo's Phantasmagoria across state lines and checking police reports, after Erin had finished filling out the arrest reports for Hugo Bucklington and Devon James. It was a day she'd really missed Patrol work. Pounding pavement and dealing with street-level bad guys felt a lot more like being real police. This was more like being a white-collar cube drone in an office filled with really unpleasant coworkers.

Something was up with the other cops in the precinct. She noticed it when she passed uniforms on the stairs, in the lobby, and in the parking garage. She was catching too many sidelong looks, hearing too many conversations that were cut off mid-sentence when she got close. Erin had seen those signs before. It meant some dirt was being passed around on her. She was marked.

It didn't make sense. At least, not unless word had gotten out about her and Carlyle. And she couldn't think how that would've happened. Whatever else he might be, Morton Carlyle was no gossip.

It was just one more puzzle, one she didn't have the energy to tackle at the end of a shift. She loaded Rolf into her Charger and drove back to her apartment, the city a blur of streetlights, headlights, and crowded cars.

The apartment's parking garage was cold and dark, matching her mood. When she parked, she just sat there for a minute and tried to collect herself. Rolf had picked up her mood and was curled up on the floor of his compartment, snout tucked under his tail.

She sighed and finally got out of the car. Her senses, numbed by the long, pointless day, were sluggish. It took her a couple of seconds to realize it was too dark in the garage. The overhead light was out. Still annoyed, not yet alarmed, she glanced up at the fixture. She saw two fluorescent bulbs, both dark.

What were the chances of two bulbs burning out at once?

A thrill of danger shot down her spine. She retreated a step to put her car at her back and reached for the door to let Rolf out. As she did, she saw a black Town Car two spaces over, in the visitor parking spot. And she saw movement in the corner of her eye.

Erin was suddenly wide awake. "Police!" she snapped, turning and going for her Glock.

She caught a quick glimpse of two big guys closing with her. Then she had her gun in hand and was bringing it up, a split second too slow. A large, strong hand grabbed her wrist and slammed her arm against her Charger's window-frame. It hurt, but she kept her grip on the gun. She drove her other hand up into the man's chin, an open palm strike. His teeth clicked together and he staggered, but didn't go down. He hit her with his free hand just under the eye. The shock of bone on bone jarred her and she saw stars.

Erin had grown up in a family of boys, with an old-school dad who'd believed in playground justice. Sean O'Reilly had taught her brothers how to fistfight. But Erin was a girl, smaller than some. He hadn't taught her how to fight fair, face-to-face. He'd taught her to fight dirty, and win.

The other guy was on her before she could wrench her gun-hand free. Erin stomped on the first man's instep as hard as she could, pivoted on his foot, and heard his hiss of pain as she jammed her hand into the second goon's throat. He gagged and grabbed his own neck.

Rolf was barking frantically, but he couldn't get into the fight. Erin's quick-release button was on her belt, but it was on her right side. That was the hand holding her Glock, the one her attacker was stubbornly holding by the wrist. She put her free elbow into his gut, just above the belt. Breath whooshed out of him. He went to his knees, but he still held on. Her arm twisted with sudden, excruciating pain.

Erin cried out and tried to pull away. She saw the other man coming in, recovered from the throat-punch. He was slipping something onto his hand. Knuckle-dusters, probably. She struggled, but the man holding her was half again her weight and a lot stronger.

The second man cocked his fist. Erin tensed, knowing she was about to get hurt.

Two gunshots exploded, so close together their echoes overlapped, rebounding off the concrete walls of the garage. The muzzle flashes lit up the darkness for just an instant. Both men froze. Then the guy holding Erin gave her right arm such a wrench that she nearly blacked out from the pain. He shoved her away. She fell, only barely getting her left arm up in time to break her fall. Dazedly, she rolled onto her side on the concrete floor. A car engine coughed to life. Headlights swung across her field of view and centered on her, blinding her.

Her arm felt funny, but its muscles obeyed her. She brought up her hand, still somehow holding her gun, and pulled the trigger twice as the car bore down on her. One of its headlights went out. Then someone grabbed her under the shoulders and hauled her roughly back behind her car. The other car went past in a rush of black metal and squealing tires.

"Did you catch one?" someone asked.

"Huh?" she mumbled.

"Are you hit?"

"No, I... I don't think so." Erin was trying to identify the voice. It was familiar.

"Then you're good, ma'am."

That last word made the connection for her. "Ian? Ian Thompson?"

But when she turned her head, her rescuer was gone.

*   *   *

A couple of uniforms showed up almost before Erin called in the attack. A neighbor had heard the gunshots and called 911. Erin wasn't surprised. The infamous Kitty Genovese murder, back in the '60s, had given New York the reputation of a city where you could be killed in broad daylight and no one would bother calling the cops, but Erin knew better. Even in that attack, a witness had called it in within a few minutes. Response time was the real problem. Fortunately, in Erin's case, a squad car had been just down the street. The siren and flashers tipped her off, so by the time the Patrol officers arrived, Erin was holding up her shield in her good hand. The attackers, however, were long gone.

"Did you get a good look at them, Detective?" one of the uniforms asked her.

She shook her head. "Too dark, too fast." There'd been that one moment of muzzle flash, but it'd been too quick to give her more than a glimpse, and the guys had been wearing watch caps and high-collared coats. "There were two of them. Caucasian. Black Lincoln Town Car. I didn't see the plates, but one of the headlights is out. The left one. It's got at least one bullet hole."

One of the cops put the vehicle description out on the radio. Erin leaned against her car, Rolf beside her. The Shepherd's hackles still bristled. He'd had to watch his partner fight it out just a few feet away, and missing the action had pissed him off.

"What're they armed with?" the radioman asked.

"Fists and brass knuckles," she said.

"What about the gun?" the other cop asked.

Erin shook her head. "That wasn't them."

"So you fired the only shots?"

She shook her head again. "There was a bystander."

"Civilian? What'd he look like?"

"I didn't get a look at his face," Erin said. That was technically true. "Look, guys, I'm tired. I'm gonna go inside and sit down. You want someone to take a statement, sure, but we can do it indoors. I'm freezing my ass off out here. And I gotta call my Lieutenant."

*   *   *

Webb wasn't happy to find work following him home, but he'd been a cop long enough to be used to it. When he answered her phone call, he sounded more bored than anything else. But as soon as Erin told him she'd been attacked, she had his undivided attention.

"Are you hurt?" he asked sharply.

"Just bruises," she said. "I got a couple good hits in."

"How many mopes?"

"Two."

"You have them in custody?"

She clenched her jaw. "No."

"How'd they get away?"

"They knocked me down. They were gonna work me over, but a bystander pulled a gun and took a couple shots at them, so they booked it. Bastards had a car waiting."

"You got uniforms on scene?"

"Yeah."

"You get the bystander's statement? And maybe take him in on a weapons charge?"

She couldn't help a cynical smile at that. The NYPD was big on getting unlicensed guns off the street. Even a Good Samaritan could get in a lot of trouble if he was packing. "No, he ran off, too. I'd say he played it smart."

"Did you recognize the bad guys?"

"Nope. They seemed like a couple of average lowlifes."

"Where was your dog while all this was going down?"

"Locked in my car. They got me just as I got out. I didn't have a chance to let him loose."

Webb paused, and Erin could practically hear the wheels turning in his head. "You thinking this was a random street crime?" he finally asked. "You were in an unmarked car. Maybe they saw a small woman, alone at night, and thought they could make an easy score."

"Maybe," she said.

"Or was it targeted? You piss anybody off recently?"

"Let's see," she said. "There's the Russian Mafia, neo-Nazi terrorists, some of the Irish Mob, maybe a few buddies of that dirty cop I put away back in October... Want me to go on?"

Webb had the decency to laugh quietly. "Okay, fair point. We've all made enemies. Tell you what. You have things under control there?"

"Sure."

"Then I'll leave you to it. If you don't think there's more to it than a mugging or attempted assault, give it to the local boys. We've got enough to worry about."

"Okay, sir."

"And if you got hit on the head, get it checked out," he finished. "Even if it feels like nothing. If you have a subdural hematoma, it can kill you in your sleep."

"I'm a first responder," she reminded him. "I know about closed-head injuries."

"Okay, okay. I worry, that's all. I've got two teenagers."

"Really? I didn't know you had family here."

"They're still in California, with their mom. They're from my first marriage."

"I'm sure they're fine."

"Oh, yeah," he said. "Teenage boys running around LA without fatherly supervision. What could possibly go wrong?"

"See you at work tomorrow, sir."

"Bright and early, O'Reilly."

* * *

Once the Patrol officers had taken her statement and gone on their way, Erin was left alone with Rolf, wondering why she hadn't told the truth.

It wasn't that she'd lied, exactly. She'd just left out a couple of things. Specifically, her opinion as to the identity of her rescuer, and her belief that the guys who'd jumped her were the same ones who'd been follower her earlier in the day. Taken together, those two opinions meant she was tangled up with the Irish Mob.

"We've got a choice," she told Rolf.

He wagged his tail, ready to get on board with whatever she suggested.

"Either we steer clear of these bastards, or we take them on."

The Shepherd cocked his head to one side, his long ears accentuating the gesture.

She smiled fondly at him and rubbed his neck. "I know what you'd say. But I don't even know whose goons are coming after me. It can't be Carlyle's guys. His man stepped in to save me. Unless..."

She trailed off as a thought struck her. Could the whole thing be a setup? Some complicated plan to win back her trust? No, that didn't make sense. That sort of plan was way too risky for a guy like Carlyle. She'd nearly been able to shoot the bad guys, and they'd been fighting her for real. She'd been in enough scuffles to know when a man was holding back on her and when he wasn't. They'd been out to cause damage.

"Okay, so Carlyle's the one guy in the O'Malleys I'm sure wasn't in on it," she said. "That means if I want answers, I need to talk to him. Damn it. I'm about out of whiskey anyway. I guess I could use a drink."

Rolf nudged her with his snout.

"Yeah, you'd better come too." She picked up his leash. He was instantly on his paws, ready and willing.

Chapter 11

Erin knew she had to be careful. The Barley Corner was a mob bar. There'd be wise guys in it. There was even a chance she'd run into the very same goons who'd just tried to beat her down. If she did, she decided, she'd haul their asses straight downtown. It'd mean being up half the night processing arrests, but it'd be worth it.

The dinner rush was in full swing, and the Corner was full. It was standing room only at the bar, the waitresses weaving through a crowd of burly men. The big-screen TVs showed some sort of rally car race, tough-looking automobiles slipping and sliding on an ice-bound course. It looked dangerous. The crowd was really into it.

Erin didn't see Carlyle, but she had a pretty good idea where he'd be. She worked her way over to his usual spot at the bar, Rolf doing a great job encouraging patrons to clear a path. There Carlyle was, an elbow resting on the bar, a glass of whiskey beside him.

With all the noise and confusion, he couldn't possibly have heard her approach, but he still turned to look at her, tipped off by a pub owner's sixth sense.

His eyes lit up with genuine surprise and delight. He stood quickly and took a step forward, then paused. His eyebrows drew together in sudden concern. Erin realized she must be a mess. She'd washed her hands and splashed some water on her face back at her apartment, but there wasn't anything she could do about the hits she'd taken. One whole side of her face felt hot and swollen, and she was pretty sure she'd have a black eye in the morning.

"Erin, what's happened?" he asked.

"Didn't your bodyguard tell you?" she shot back.

It wasn't often that Carlyle looked confused, but Erin was too tired, beat-up, and irritated to enjoy it. She didn't give him much chance to answer. "Look," she said. "We need to talk. Somewhere private."

"Aye," he agreed. "I'm thinking we do." He led the way through the crowd to the door to the back stairs.

The moment the door closed behind her and Rolf, she turned on Carlyle. "Okay, start talking."

"Would you care to come upstairs? We can be more comfortable."

"I don't want comfort. I want answers!"

"Perhaps I can supply them," he said quietly. "Provided you begin with the questions."

Erin took a deep breath. They were at the bottom of the stairs to his apartment suite, maybe eighteen inches separating them. Rolf watched her carefully, waiting for orders.

"Okay," she began. "What do you know about a couple of goons, driving a Lincoln Town Car?"

"That's not much to go on."

"They jumped me in my apartment's garage after work."

"Are you badly injured?" He raised a hand as if to touch her.

She shrugged him away. "I'm fine. Your boy Ian bailed me out. He shot at them and they booked it. They tried to run me down on the way out, but he dragged me behind cover. Then he ran off, too. So what gives?"

Carlyle was thinking hard. His eyes didn't give much away, but she'd had some practice reading him. "I've not spoken with Ian this evening," he said at last. "What did he say to you?"

"He asked if I'd been hit, then said I was good, and then he was gone."

Carlyle smiled thinly. "That's certainly the sort of thing he might say. You say this lad left immediately?"

"Yeah. Why'd he run off?"

"You'd have to ask him. But I imagine he mightn't wish to be involved in your investigation."

"If that was what he wanted, why'd he shoot at a couple of thugs right in front of me?"

"These men who attacked you. You say they ran away, so I assume they were able to move. Were either of them wounded?"

"I gave them something to remember," she said grimly.

"I mean, were they shot?"

"No, I don't think so."

"Then if that lad was Ian, he wasn't shooting to kill."

"How do you know?"

"Ian doesn't shoot at people. And he doesn't miss, not at close range."

"Bullshit," Erin said flatly. "Everybody misses in a gunfight. You want to know the stats when the NYPD start shooting? Sixteen percent hit rate. With all our training. And that's at close-range, mostly inside ten meters."

"Nonetheless," Carlyle said. "Ian's a hardened combat veteran, with a steady hand and a very keen eye. If he'd meant to hit your assailants, they'd not have survived. Or, at the least, they'd have been in no condition to run."

"You're saying he fired warning shots, to scare them away?"

Carlyle shrugged. "I've your word it was he who came to your aid. In that case, if your attackers are still breathing, it's because he wanted them to be." He held her eyes with his own. "Erin, darling, let's have no misunderstandings here. You know the life I lead, the lads with whom I associate. So I hope you'll take my meaning when I say there's no man on Manhattan Island more dangerous than Ian Thompson."

Erin matched him stare for stare. "That's the guy you've got watching my back?"

"Aye."

"Jesus Christ. Who's coming after me?"

"The word's gone out that you're connected," he said. "The sad truth, Erin, is that at this point, the lads in my world don't much care whether you and I are truly involved with one another or not. They're assuming we are. Too much has happened already, too many coincidences. You've saved my life one time too many. And there's the matter of Thomas O'Malley."

"That was a clean arrest," she objected. It had been a cold case, a murder the nephew of Carlyle's boss had ordered years ago, carried out by a dirty cop. Erin had dug out the mole in the department and flipped him, which had led to Tommy Jay O'Malley's incarceration. It'd been a lot of things, but "clean" probably wasn't the best word for what had happened.

Carlyle sighed. "Tommy Jay's abrupt departure left a gap in my organization. I've been elevated to his former position. Combined with your remarkable tendency to turn up to protect me at opportune moments, there's a pattern of behavior."

"But if these guys think I'm working with you, why are they coming after me?" Erin demanded. "Are these jerks O'Malley goons, or somebody else?"

"If you're in the game, it's fair play to them, as far as they're concerned," he said. "Whoever they may be. Being a copper may buy you a little protection, but not much. I'd assume they've some connection to the much-lamented Tommy Jay, were I a gambler."

"You are a gambler," she reminded him.

"Indeed," he replied. "Do you know what these lads intended, when they accosted you?"

"They were looking for a punching bag," Erin said dryly.

"It wasn't an attempted hit, then," he said.

"No," she agreed. "They'd have used guns if they wanted me dead."

"So perhaps your badge does still shield you."

"Not much," she echoed him. "They made a solid effort at running me down on their way out. So what's your stake in this?"

"Mine?" He looked surprised. "I've told you. You're my interest in this affair. I can offer you some protection of my own, perhaps work with you to deal with these miscreants."

"Your way, or mine?"

"Which would you prefer?"

She glared at him. "I'm a cop, dammit."

"Then I assume you'll be taking Ian in for questioning."

Erin blinked. She opened her mouth, but nothing came out.

"You recognized him, but you didn't put his name to this business?" Carlyle asked quietly.

Erin didn't answer, because she didn't have a reason why she hadn't given Ian's name to the NYPD. It'd been an instinctive response. Maybe because he was an associate of Carlyle's, and dragging him in might've pulled the whole business with Carlyle out into the open. She wasn't compromised by her thing with Carlyle, she reminded herself. Except that by keeping his guy out of the incident, wasn't she proving exactly the opposite?

Carlyle was watching her with his keen blue eyes, and she had the feeling he was guessing most of what was going through her head.

"So, what you're saying is, I'm screwed either way, so I might as well come in with you because I haven't got anything to lose?"

"I'm saying nothing of the sort. I want you to come in with me because I want to be with you, nothing more. I was simply pointing out the tactical advantages."

"Are you ever not playing an angle?" she demanded. "Are you ever unreasonable?"

"Aye," he said. "When it comes to the people I care for, I can be the most unreasonable man on this Earth."

"Is that supposed to impress me?"

He shrugged again. "I don't care if I impress you, but I'd like you to believe me."

"And trust you?"

"Aye, that too."

"Well, I don't."

His jaw tightened. "I'm sorry to hear that. How might I convince you otherwise?"

Erin shook her head. "I don't know."

"Then we're at a temporary impasse, you and I," he said.

"Looks like it."

"There's nothing I can do for you?"

"I could use a drink."

He smiled slightly. "Now that I can easily provide. You did tell me you were low on whiskey when last we spoke. You'll take a bottle, with my compliments?"

"This doesn't buy you anything," she reminded him.

"I know. But if it pleases you, it's well worth the price."

She put a hand on the doorknob. Almost against her will, she added, "See you around, Carlyle."

"I'll look forward to it, Erin."

Chapter 12

Erin was too wired on residual adrenaline to feel the lack of sleep. She knew from experience that she'd pay a price down the line, but that was a problem for another day. She went for her morning run, same as always. Every step of the way, she looked for threats. But either the thugs had been scared off, or they were keeping out of sight. She and Rolf didn't see anything suspicious, not even a glimpse of her dangerous guardian angel.

The New York streets were eerily normal; cold, plain concrete and asphalt. It was hard to believe New Year's had been only a couple of days ago. The city had recovered and gone back to business as usual.

Vic and Lieutenant Webb were already up in Major Crimes when Erin arrived. Webb gave her a concerned look. Vic just grinned.

"You got mugged, huh?" he said.

"Yeah," she replied.

"Stupid SOBs," was his verdict. "You ready to do some police work?"

"Giving me orders? I outrank you," she reminded him.

"And I outrank both of you, put together," Webb said. "All three of you, counting the dog. Neshenko found Grimes's hotel reservation. I got the warrant, first thing this morning. CSU's gonna meet us there."

"What're we looking for?" Erin asked.

"Anything that'll give us a handle on this case," Webb said.

"Which hotel?" she asked.

"Wanna guess?" Vic answered.

She gave him a look.

"The Hilton," Webb said. "Same one you interviewed Miller at."

"Coincidence?" Erin wondered aloud.

"I've heard of coincidence," Webb said. "I stopped believing in it about the same time I found out Santa wasn't real."

"Santa's not real?" Vic echoed. "Damn."

"What's the matter?" Erin asked. "Lose a bit of your childhood?"

"It's not that," he said as they started for the door. "I was just thinking of all the shit I could've got up to when I was little, if I hadn't been worried about that fat bastard looking over my shoulder."

*   *   *

They didn't go to the penthouse this time. Kathy Grimes had been staying in a much more modest room, not even a suite, on the twenty-third floor.

"What about Whitaker?" Erin asked as the elevator carried them up.

"What about him?" Webb answered.

"He staying in the same room?"

"Nope," Vic said. "His room was down the hall. Guess their on-stage chemistry didn't extend to real life."

"Either that, or he was worried she'd pick his pockets while he was asleep," Erin said. "I wouldn't give that girl a room key, either."

The CSU team was waiting in the hallway with a concierge. He looked over Webb's warrant, nodded, and opened the door for them.

The room was simple but classy, dominated by a king-size bed across from a TV stand. A big picture window ran the length of the opposite wall, giving a good view of Manhattan. A chair and end table stood between the bed and the window. Erin reflected that detectives spent an awful lot of time in hotel rooms. She wondered whether people in hotels were more likely to commit crimes, or to be victims. It was the sort of stat Kira Jones would know, she thought with a twinge of sadness.

"Gloves, people," Webb reminded them.

Vic rolled his eyes.

The advantage of searching a hotel room was that there weren't really all that many places to hide something. Kathy Grimes had been living out of a suitcase, and she didn't have a lot of belongings. Clearly, she was used to being on the road.

Erin drifted over to the suitcase, which was being examined by one of the CSU guys. "Looks a little rumpled," she observed. Clothes were tossed around in it, almost carelessly.

"Yeah," the evidence tech said. "Looks like someone already went through this."

Erin nodded and stepped back. She did the old trick her dad had taught her, closing her eyes, taking a deep breath, and opening them again, taking in the scene with fresh eyes. This time, she wasn't looking for something hidden. She was looking for signs of a burglary.

The bed had been made up by the maid, so it was neat and tidy. So was everything else in the room. Erin took her time, letting her eyes wander from one thing to another.

Then she saw it. The chair by the window had a set of small, circular depressions in the carpet that didn't quite line up with the chair legs.

"That's been moved," she said quietly, pointing to the chair.

Vic followed her gesture. "Yeah," he agreed. "Could be housekeeping."

"Might not be," she said. She knelt and examined the chair. The upholstery didn't look to have been tampered with. There was no obvious reason to have moved the chair a few inches. She sat back on her heels and looked around again.

The slightly lower angle gave her a different view of the carpet. She saw a shallower set of depressions at the window, near one side.

"Over there," she said. "Someone moved the chair."

"To get a window view?" Webb suggested.

"No," Vic said. He was catching Erin's drift. "There isn't a good view from this angle. This looks more like..."

"Like someone was using the chair as a step-stool," Erin finished. She hurried to the curtain and stuck her head behind it. "I think something's wedged in there," she said, looking up. "But I can't reach it." She could hardly see it; it was hidden behind the curtain's upper guard, taped in place where it was almost impossible to spot.

Vic, almost a foot taller than Erin, was able to get a hand high enough. He pulled down a manila envelope.

"What's inside?" Webb asked.

Wordlessly, Vic upended the envelope on the bed. Tight-wrapped bundles of twenty-dollar bills poured out onto the sheet.

Webb whistled softly. "Whoever searched this place, they didn't find this."

"I miss the old days," Vic said.

"What old days are those?" Erin asked.

"The days when cash didn't make it into the evidence lockers."

Erin just shook her head. "You are so full of shit." Vic talked trash, but he was as honest as any cop she knew.

"Okay, let's bag it," Webb said. "We'll count it back at the precinct." He turned to the CSU techs. "I want this place dusted, especially the suitcase. If Grimes was killed over this cash, maybe the perp was the one who searched her stuff, looking for it."

*   *   *

In the precinct, they would've walked right past the couple waiting by the front desk. But the man stood up and stepped into their path. He was a big guy, broad-shouldered, thick around the middle. He was holding a Detroit Tigers baseball cap in his rough-looking hands.

"Excuse me," he said. "They told me to wait for a Lieutenant Webb. That you?"

Webb stopped. "Yes, sir," he said. "What can I do for you?"

"I'm Bernie Grimes," the man said. "This is my wife, Loretta." He indicated the woman he'd been sitting next to. She had a grandmotherly look, sporting a beauty-salon pile of gray curls. The woman raised a hand in a vague gesture that might have been a greeting, or just an acknowledgment.

"We just got in," Grimes went on. "I was hoping... I mean, I thought..." He looked down into the baseball cap, maybe hoping to find some inspiration in it. "They told us you've got our little girl here. Can... can we see her?"

Erin, remembering the hard-nosed way he'd talked about Kathy on the phone, was a little surprised. But death was an emotionally complicated experience, one which police officers often saw at second hand. When she'd first talked to Mr.

Grimes, the reality hadn't yet sunk in that his daughter was dead. Apparently, in the meantime, it had hit him, and hit him hard. She felt a pang of sympathy.

"Mr. Grimes," Webb said carefully, "Miss Grimes's remains are being examined for any information that will help us bring her killer to justice. I would strongly advise against viewing her at this time. I'm sure you understand."

Grimes stepped forward and spoke in a much lower voice, trying to keep his words out of earshot of his wife. "How bad is it? I mean..."

"You don't want to remember her like this, sir," Erin said quietly.

He thought about it and nodded slowly. "Maybe not," he said. His shoulders slumped. "We just thought... I mean... God, I taught her to ride a tricycle. Seems like last week." His face started to crumple in slow motion.

Loretta stood and put an arm around her husband.

"Mrs. Grimes?" Erin asked gently.

"Yes?" the other woman said. Her voice was distant. She was staring right past Erin at nothing in particular.

"Your husband told me you'd spoken with Kathy about her boyfriend. What can you tell me about him?"

Kathy's mother blinked slowly. "She said he was... ambitious. That he was going to go places, and she'd go with him. Once they got some money together."

"What was his name?"

Loretta's brow wrinkled. "I'm not sure."

Erin didn't accept that. She knew from personal experience that her own mother wouldn't let a boyfriend stay a secret for long. "Please, try to remember. Take your time."

"Lucas, maybe... or Louis," Mrs. Grimes said. She nodded. "Yes, that's it. Louis."

"Louis Miller?" Webb prompted.

"I don't know. She didn't tell me his last name."

"We already know about him," Vic muttered.

Erin held up a hand to shut him up. "Kathy was trying to get money? She was planning to run off with Louis?"

"That's what she said," Mrs. Grimes said.

"Did she say where she was going to get the money?" Erin asked.

The woman shook her head.

"Kat could always find money," Mr. Grimes said. "Her gifts were her smile... and her quick fingers."

*   *   *

"Does that make Miller more of a suspect, or less?" Vic wondered aloud. They were back in Major Crimes, looking at the whiteboard. The Grimes family was talking to the victim-assistance coordinator downstairs, working through the bureaucracy of death in America.

"Both," Webb sighed. "O'Reilly, did Miller indicate he was planning to run off with Grimes?"

"No," she said. "He didn't seem that broken up by what happened. Hell, by the end of the conversation, he was hitting on me."

"Really?" Vic looked interested. "What'd you say?"

Erin gave him a look. "I told him where to stick his magic wand."

Vic snorted.

"Okay," Webb said quietly, without looking away from the board. "Whoever did this, it was personal. You'd have to really hate someone to do something like this."

"Or love them," Erin said.

"Yeah," Webb said. He rubbed his chin with one hand. The other was fidgeting with an unlit cigarette. "If they'd let me smoke in here, I swear, my clearance rate would go up twenty percent." He turned to look at his detectives. "Go on, get out of here. Clear your heads, get some lunch in you, and come back with ideas. That's an order."

Chapter 13

"You want to grab some takeout?" Vic asked.

"No, thanks," Erin said. "You go on."

"You okay?" he asked, pausing and looking closely at her.

"Fine."

He stepped in front of her. "Hey, did those jack-offs tune you up worse than you said? Look, we can go after them. You must've got a quick look at them, at least. We can ask around. I got a couple guys I can talk to, maybe get a lead."

"Aw, Vic... are you offering to help beat the shit out of some guys? That's the sweetest thing anyone's said to me today."

He smiled sourly. "Well? Whaddaya say?"

"Rain check."

"Okay. You change your mind, let me know." He glanced at Rolf. "Can't let Fuzzy here have all the fun."

Rolf returned the look coolly.

"I'm gonna call my sister-in-law," Erin said.

"Sure thing. See you in an hour, when you get tired of dealing with civilians." Vic headed off.

Erin took out her phone. Running into Kathy's parents had put family on her mind.

"Erin!" Michelle said when she picked up, sounding genuinely delighted. "Guess who's here?"

"Shelley, I have no idea."

"Your dad came down for the day."

"Really?" Erin's spirits lifted. "You doing anything for lunch?"

"Of course we are!"

"Oh." Disappointment came down on her.

"We're going out with you, silly," Michelle said. "My treat. We're actually not that far from your precinct. Your dad was planning to drop in and say hi. How about the Odeon, on Broadway? We can meet you there in, say, fifteen?"

"Sure," Erin said.

"And you can tell me all about that mystery man from New Year's," Michelle said mischievously. She hung up before Erin could protest.

Erin looked at her K-9. "You got my back, big guy?"

Rolf wagged his tail.

*　　*　　*

The Odeon had been one of the go-to eateries in Lower Manhattan back in the '90s and remained a standby, a classic downtown bistro on the northern edge of Tribeca. Erin was worried about getting a quick seat, but Michelle, her kids, and Erin's dad had gotten there a few minutes ahead of her and had lucked into a table. Erin and Rolf saw them the moment they passed under the red awning, Michelle standing up to wave to her.

Anna and Patrick clustered around Rolf, who was proudly wearing his bulletproof vest. Ever since the attack in the garage, Erin had been paranoid about going out in the open, so they were ready for anything.

Sean O'Reilly stood as Erin approached and looked her over. The patriarch of the O'Reilly clan was the same as ever, a little grayer in the mustache maybe, and a little stouter, but still the calm, reassuring veteran cop of Erin's childhood.

"How you doing, kiddo?" he asked, looking sharply at her battered face.

"I'm good, Dad," she said, giving him a quick hug.

"Nice shiner."

She reflexively touched the swelling around her eye. "You should see the other guy."

"What happened?" Michelle asked, staring at Erin's black eye.

"The Job," Erin replied.

Sean nodded silently. He'd worked Patrol and been in enough fights to need no further explanation.

"What's good here?" Erin asked, changing the subject.

"I'm getting the Baby Kale Caesar Salad," Michelle said.

"I think Erin was asking about food," Sean said. "I'm getting the BLT."

"Mommy?" Anna asked. "What's steak tar-tare?"

"Tartare," Michelle said. "You don't want that, dear."

"But what is it?"

"It's like a hamburger," Erin said. "Except raw."

"Raw?" Anna wrinkled her nose. "That's gross!"

"Some people like it," Sean said.

"Do you, Grandpa?"

"I like my meat," he said, pretending to think it over. "But I like to know it's dead before I put it in my mouth."

"On that note," Erin said, "I think I'll get a burger."

"I'm getting a puppy," Anna announced.

"For lunch?" Sean asked in mock horror.

"No, Grandpa!" Anna said. "Mommy said it'll be good for me. Having a pet fosters responsibility."

"That's important," Erin said. "What kind of dog?"

"It's not decided yet," Michelle said. "Her father and I are negotiating. We're looking into shelters and rescue organizations. Why spend a thousand bucks on some harebrained, inbred purebred from some puppy mill when there's some sweet mutt who needs a home?"

"It's okay, partner," Erin said to Rolf. "She's not talking about you."

Rolf gave her a mournful look more suited to a basset hound than a German Shepherd.

After they'd ordered, Michelle leaned forward. "Okay, sis," she said. "Let's have it."

"What?"

"Don't play innocent. Who's the guy?"

"What guy?" Sean asked.

"If I didn't tell you at New Year's," Erin said, "after I'd had a couple of drinks, what makes you think getting me to talk in front of my dad would be easier?"

"It's okay, kiddo," Sean said. "Face it, I've never liked any of your boyfriends. So there's no pressure. I'm sure to hate this one, too."

"I don't have a boyfriend!"

"I do," Anna announced.

"You do?" Erin echoed.

"That's right," Anna said, with the certainty that came with being nine years old. "He sits two rows in front of me in math."

"What's his name?" Erin asked, glad to divert attention.

"Brian Burkhart. He wears big plastic glasses, he can hold his breath for almost a minute, and he gave me a live frog just before Thanksgiving."

Erin nodded soberly. "Sounds like a keeper."

"So. How's work?" Sean asked, recognizing Erin wasn't going to open up on the boyfriend front. "IAB leaving you alone?"

"That's cleared up." Erin had been under investigation by Internal Affairs, but had gotten out from under by finding a genuinely dirty cop. That'd been one of the most unpleasant things she'd had to do, and she hurried to change the subject. "You hear about the theater thing?"

"Yeah," he said. "It was all over the news. All over the theater, too, from the sound of it."

"Careful," Michelle said, flicking her gaze over her kids. "Easy on the detail."

"You crack it yet?" Sean asked.

"Not yet," Erin said.

"Any suspects?"

"Everywhere we look. The girl made enemies."

"We've all got enemies," Sean said. "You've got them, I've got them, I'll bet even Anna's got enemies. You got enemies, kiddo?"

"Yes," Anna said. "Molly Perkins and Madison Carver. They're..." she leaned forward, "itches with a capital B."

"Anna!" Michelle exclaimed, horrified.

Erin put a napkin to her face to cover her grin, and saw her dad smiling through his mustache.

"But none of those people are gonna kill you," Sean said. "And the way this perp did it..."

"It's a statement," Erin said.

"Loud and clear," he agreed. "We've both seen the usual type of homicide. Bullets, knives, back-alley stuff. Your average Joe gets pissed, wants to whack someone, this isn't how he does it."

"This was theatrical," Erin said. "I know."

"So you're looking for someone theatrical," Sean said. "Forget motive. There's motive everywhere. And forget means.

What you're looking for here is style. This is a crime with a signature."

"Dad? Why didn't you ever make detective?"

"I liked wearing blue," he said. "Couldn't get used to a suit."

"Signature," Erin said. "You're right. This is a guy who wanted it to be as public as possible. He wanted witnesses. Hundreds of them. This guy's confident."

"Yes, he is," Sean said. "That's how you catch him."

"Confidence?"

"Yeah. Because this guy will need people to know it was him, sooner or later. There's clues, if you know where to look. I think this guy wants revenge more than he wants to get away with it."

"I hope you're right, Dad," she said. "Because right now, he's doing a pretty good job of getting away with it."

"Mommy?" Anna asked. She was looking at the menu again.

"Yes, dear?"

"What's ca... calam..."

"Calamari," Michelle said. "It's squid."

"People eat squid?"

"Sometimes."

"What's it like?"

"Imagine a mouthful of rubber bands," Sean said.

"I don't understand grown-up food," Anna said.

"Neither do the grown-ups," Erin said. "We just get better at faking it."

*   *   *

"Well?" Vic asked.

"Well what?" Erin replied.

"You solve the case? Get a blinding insight? Find wisdom? See the face of God?"

Erin shook her head. "I figure I was doing well just getting a burger that was cooked."

"I sent you for food and ideas, people," Webb said.

"One out of two ain't bad," Vic said.

"We're looking for a criminal with style," Erin said, remembering her dad's words.

"Go on," Webb said.

"Two people have told me that," she said. "Louis Miller said Kathy would've appreciated the theatricality of her death."

"You think that's true?" Webb asked.

She shrugged. "I don't think it matters what I think. I'm not the intended audience."

"No," Vic said. "Those poor bastards in the theater were."

"I'm not sure about that," Erin said. "I think maybe the message wasn't meant for the people who were there."

"The hell it wasn't," Vic said. "Those kids are gonna support New York's therapy industry for years."

"Hold on, Neshenko," Webb said. "O'Reilly might be on to something. You think this was like a mob hit? A statement killing?"

"It's one hell of a statement," she said. In her mind's eye, she saw Carlyle nod approvingly. The thought pleased her.

"So who is the audience?" Webb asked.

"The obvious one is Ron Whitaker," she said.

"Front row seat," Vic observed. "It's a good way to trash his career, kill his assistant, wreck his self-confidence."

"So, you're thinking Whitaker might be the real target," Webb said. "And Grimes was incidental?"

"If someone wanted to send him a message, it's a great way to do it," Erin said.

"If you don't mind turning a girl into hamburger to make your point," Vic said.

"I shouldn't have told you what I had for lunch," Erin said.

Webb turned to the board. "So, who wants Whitaker scared? Neshenko, run his financials. See if he owed money to anybody. If loan sharks wanted to scare him, they might've decided to hit someone close to him."

"I was just thinking we needed more suspects," Vic muttered.

"You got a problem doing police work, Neshenko?"

Vic stopped. He slowly turned to face his commanding officer. "No, sir, I've got no problem doing police work." He spoke very distinctly, emphasizing each word.

"There something else you have to say, Detective?"

A muscle twitched in Vic's cheek. "How'd I get on your shit list? Sir?"

Webb put his hands on his hips. "You'd better either stop talking right now, or explain yourself," he said in a dangerously quiet voice.

"I used to work ESU," Vic snapped. "In the Bronx. I've kicked down doors and taken down hard collars. I've been in fistfights, knife fights, and gunfights. I've been shot. What the hell am I doing riding a goddamn desk all day? You and Erin go running all over the Five Boroughs, and I'm still here with my thumb up my ass, every damn day. You want to tell me why?"

"You done?" Webb asked, still speaking softly.

Vic thought it over. "One more thing."

"And that is?"

"If you weren't hiding behind that lieutenant's shield, I'd kick your ass. Sir."

"Okay," Webb said. "You've had your say. Now sit your ass down." Suddenly, his voice cracked like a whip. "That's an order."

Vic stood there another moment. Erin thought, for those few seconds, that Detective Neshenko was considering quitting the NYPD in some spectacular way. The anger radiated off him like an almost physical force. Very, very slowly, he lowered himself into his chair.

"Now listen to me," Webb said. "You're a damn good detective, Neshenko. How many shootouts have you been in, the past six months?"

Vic considered.

"How many men have you killed?" Webb went on, when he didn't get an immediate answer.

"Three... maybe four."

"You're not sure how many gunfights you've been in, or how many people you've killed," Webb said. "That seem like the normal police experience to you?"

Vic didn't answer.

"I've lost track of the number of Critical Incident reports this squad has filed," Webb said. "By my count, since we became operational, we've shot and killed five perps, wounded another half-dozen plus, and sustained numerous line-of-duty injuries. You've been in the front lines the whole way. You don't have to tell me you're a tough SOB. I know that. Hell, the greater New York metropolitan area knows that by now. But all that shit takes a toll on you."

"I've passed my psych evaluations," Vic growled.

"I know," Webb said. "You wouldn't be on duty at all if you hadn't. But you're a pressure cooker, Neshenko. I'm giving you a chance to get your head right, before you go back on the sharp end."

"What about Erin?"

"What about her?"

"Everything you told me is true about her, too. Aren't you worried she's gonna go crazy and start popping off rounds?"

"Now that you mention it," Webb said, "I am. You gonna go crazy on me, O'Reilly?"

"Wasn't planning on it, sir," Erin said.

"Doesn't matter," Webb said. "Given the choice, I'd bench the both of you until spring. But I don't have that choice. Because my only other detective went back to Internal Affairs and left us a man down."

"Kira's a woman," Vic reminded him.

"Shut up," Webb said. "My point is, we're thin on the ground here. Jones was the best desk jockey I've ever had, but she doesn't work here anymore, so the rest of us have to pick up the slack. I'm sorry if your feelings are hurt, Neshenko. Tell you what. I'll make you an offer, out of the goodness of my heart."

"I'm all ears, sir."

"You and I are going to go back to the theater, take a look around, see if we missed anything. We'll talk to Whitaker again, try to figure out who might be leaning on him. If he's already scared, you might be able to tip him over the edge, shake something loose. O'Reilly will stay here and look into Whitaker's money. And, as a bonus, I won't give you a rip for your blatant insubordination."

"In exchange for what?" Vic asked. He didn't trust generosity that came down the chain of command.

"If you ever, I mean ever talk to a superior officer like that again, whether it's me, Captain Holliday, the Commissioner, almighty God, whoever, I will personally see to it that you spend the rest of your professional career on Staten Island, in a uniform that doesn't fit you, guarding a crosswalk. Do I make myself clear?"

"Crystal, sir," Vic said. But there was a bounce in his step when he stood up.

Erin watched them go, fuming internally. They were going to check up on her idea. Vic was being rewarded for insubordination, while she was left holding the fort. But she knew better than to get in the middle of that situation. She'd probably be safer away from her squad-mates while they cooled off.

Chapter 14

"Follow the money" was one of the first rules of police work, but it was one of Erin's least favorite tasks. She liked chasing down her prey. She and Rolf were at their best on the street. But their noses and instincts didn't work online.

She stared at her computer screen, daring it to reveal the secrets of Ronald Whitaker's bank accounts. All she saw was her own reflection, shadowy and distant.

"Hey... Erin?"

"Yeah?" she replied, without looking up. The voice was familiar enough that it didn't startle her at first. Then her brain caught up with her and she did a double-take. "Kira?"

Kira Jones, one-time Major Crimes Detective, now working a desk upstairs at Internal Affairs, came hesitantly out of the stairwell.

Erin hardly recognized her. The other woman had a fondness for edgy fashion; this was the first time Erin had ever seen her in formal office attire. She hadn't re-applied her hair dye, either. Her hair was still dark red toward the tips, but had started growing in black.

"Help you?" Erin asked. She didn't know quite what to say. Kira was her friend, or had been. Now she was the working cop's boogeyman.

"I thought I'd come down, see how you were doing," Kira said. She tried a cautious smile. "Remind myself how real cops do things."

"So, the Bloodhound let you off leash?" Erin asked. That was the nickname for Kira's boss, Lieutenant Keane. Everyone at Precinct 8, except maybe Captain Holliday, was scared of Keane.

"He's at a meeting, offsite."

"He know you're down here?" Erin meant it as a sour joke.

"No." Kira didn't smile.

"The rest of the squad's out," Erin said.

"I know."

Erin narrowed her eyes. "Keeping pretty close tabs on us, aren't you."

"Take it easy, Erin. I want to help."

"That why you bailed on us? Because you wanted to help?" The words just slipped out.

Kira winced. "It wasn't like that, Erin."

"That so? Because I was there, and that's kind of what it looked like."

Kira shook her head. "I didn't want to leave, Erin. Jesus, I know, I'm a coward. Okay? I was scared. You happy to hear me say it? I didn't want to die, and if I kept working with the team, that was gonna happen."

"Cut the drama," Erin said harshly. "None of us have gotten killed."

"That's not what I meant," Kira said, coming closer and dropping her voice. "Listen to me, okay? That ambush with the Russians really fucked me up. I couldn't sleep for weeks. Nightmares, flashbacks, the whole works. I tried pills, I tried booze, I tried friggin' therapy. Then you know what? I ended up sitting in my bathroom at two in the morning one night, holding my service piece, wondering how it'd feel if I just shoved the thing in my mouth. That maybe it'd be worth it if it'd just make me stop being scared. I couldn't take it anymore. That's why I left. It was killing me."

"Jesus," Erin said quietly. Her anger was gone as quickly as it had flared up. "Kira, I... I didn't know."

"The crazy thing is, now that it's gone, I miss it, a little," Kira said. She pulled Vic's chair away from his desk and sat down facing Erin. "I feel like I just kicked a heroin habit. I know it'd ruin my life to go back, but sometimes I miss the high, too."

Erin managed a slight smile. "Yeah, I get that."

"Working for Keane... it's different," Kira said. "He's smart. He just knows things about people. He can read a guy better than anyone I know. He's a damn good cop, and he's not bad to work for. But... shit, I don't know. That's enough about me anyway. I didn't come down here for confession."

"You're not Catholic anyway," Erin remembered. "Lapsed Unitarian, wasn't it?"

"Yeah. Like my mom."

"So why are you here?"

"I wanted to give you a heads-up."

"About what?"

"Rumors."

"What sort of rumors?"

"About you."

Erin felt her stomach tighten. "Who's spreading them?"

Kira licked her lips. "I don't know. I haven't tried to nail down the source. But they're specific, and it feels like... like something out of a political campaign."

"How do you mean?"

"It's a smear job." Kira wrinkled her nose. "Someone's trying to discredit you in the department."

"Christ," Erin said in disgust. "This is so middle school."

"No shit. But you need to hear it, if you haven't already."

"What's the point?"

Kira leaned in. "Because someone's trying to hurt you, Erin. One of ours."

"Okay, let's hear it."

Kira extended her index finger. "First, people are saying you're a mole for IAB."

"I know," Erin said. "Ever since you and I nailed the O'Malleys' inside man."

Another finger joined the first. "Second, word is you've got a hook which got you your promotion to Second Grade. Detectives don't usually get bumped up that fast. You don't have political pull, so the story is that you're screwing around with one of the higher-ups in the department."

"Like Holliday?" Erin said in disbelief. "I hardly ever even talk to the guy!"

"Talking isn't the point," Kira said. She added a third finger. "And third, you're helping take down particular criminals to help members of a specific organization."

"So I'm doing hit jobs for the O'Malleys?" Erin asked. "That's what you mean?"

"Yeah."

Erin took a deep breath. "So, let me get this straight. According to this son of a bitch, whoever they are, I'm a dirty cop who spies on our own people, works for the Mob, and screws her boss. Am I missing anything?"

Kira nodded. "That's about it."

"But no one's filed a formal report with your office about any of this?"

"That's the funny thing," Kira said. "We hear anything even close to this about anyone in the precinct, we check it out. But Keane doesn't have a file open on you."

"That's good news," Erin said. Then she caught the look in Kira's eye. "Isn't it?"

"I don't understand it," Kira said. "And that makes it bad news. Keane seems to be just ignoring you."

"Maybe he knows I'm a good cop."

"He doesn't ignore anybody. If he pretends not to see you, it means he's really paying extra attention. He might be getting ready to pounce."

"Wouldn't you know about an investigation?"

"Maybe. Maybe not." Kira sat back and spread her hands. "I'm just one of his people. He doesn't tell me everything. But I'm telling you, there's no official file."

Erin sighed. "Okay, thanks for the heads-up. I don't know what I can do about it, though."

"I don't either. Just thought you should know." Kira stood up. "Sorry for bothering you. And... I miss you, Erin."

Her face had gone softer. Erin was surprised, and touched. "We miss you here, too."

"Really?"

"Yeah. None of the rest of us can work financial records like you can."

"That what you're doing here?" Kira leaned forward and glanced at Erin's screen, interested.

"Yeah. This is the magician, the one whose assistant got sawed in half."

"I know about that, saw it on the news. Gross. Hey, you mind?"

Erin gladly wheeled her chair to one side. Kira started tapping keys, navigating banking subsystems with the ease of long practice.

"Shouldn't you be getting back to IAB?" Erin asked after a few minutes.

"In a second," Kira said absently. "What're we looking for?"

"Any irregularities. Large deposits or withdrawals, money laundering, that sort of thing."

"Hmm. Well, it looks like he's got an unpredictable flow through his bank accounts," Kira said. "Makes sense, if he's getting paid by the job, city to city. Normal expenditures... except for this, here."

"What?" Erin followed Kira's gesture.

"Three withdrawals, ten grand each, a couple days apart."

"Thirty thousand total?"

"Yeah, but in small enough chunks not to trigger a CTR."

"Kira, I'm a street cop. I don't know bank lingo."

"Currency Transaction Report," Kira explained. "Anything over ten thousand, banks automatically generate it. If it looks weird to the bank, an SAR can be filed. That's a Suspicious Activities Report. If that happens, the account holder is notified and can block the transaction."

"So, the reason for withdrawals like this would be to avoid attention from the bank?" Erin asked.

Kira nodded. "Which would only make sense if the account holder was doing something they didn't want people to notice, or maybe if someone else was manipulating the account."

"You mean bank fraud?"

"They could be draining his accounts."

"Where were these transactions?"

"Sterling National, on West 39th."

Erin scanned the computer screen. "With the last withdrawal happening on New Year's Eve." She jumped to her feet. "I'll check it out. Thanks, Kira!"

"Don't mention it," Kira said. "Hey, be careful, okay?"

"Always am." Erin was heading for the door. Rolf trotted beside her, eager for action.

"I didn't mean with the criminals."

Erin paused. "Yeah, I know. And thanks, again."

"We should get together sometime," Kira said. "Grab a drink, maybe. If you're willing to hang with an IA officer."

Erin nodded. "I'd like that."

*   *   *

On the way to the bank, Erin gave Webb a quick call to let him know what she was doing. She checked her rear-view mirrors constantly, wondering whether she was still being followed. If those two goons were chasing her, they were being careful about it. Remembering what Carlyle had said about Ian, her shadowy guardian angel, Erin didn't blame them. She felt a little like the bait on the end of a fishhook.

Her mind was spinning with what Kira had told her. If her former squad-mate was right, someone inside the NYPD was trying to sabotage her. She couldn't even begin to guess why. Jealousy? Spite? Loyalty to the dirty cop she'd brought down? Or something else?

It was a relief to shove her personal worries to the back of her brain and turn her thoughts to a simple subject like murder. She walked into Sterling National Bank, Rolf trotting beside her, and flashed her shield to a teller.

She ended up in a manager's office. He was about her dad's age, well-dressed and very polite. She accepted a cup of coffee and took a seat. Rolf sat next to her chair and kept his eyes on Erin.

"What can I do for the police department, Detective?" the manager asked.

"Sir, over the past week, there have been three withdrawals, totaling thirty thousand dollars, made from this bank," she said. "These were made from the account of a Ronald Whitaker, who is a person of interest in an ongoing homicide investigation. All I need to determine is whether Mr. Whitaker himself made these withdrawals, or whether someone else did it in his place."

"Detective," he said, "we require photographic identification for every cash withdrawal. The individual requesting the transaction would have to have been a holder of the account. Is anyone else named on Mr. Whitaker's account?"

"No, sir."

He spread his hands on his desk. "Then the customer must have been Mr. Whitaker."

"Would it be possible to examine security footage?" she asked. "Just for confirmation purposes?"

"We would be happy to accommodate a court order..." he began.

Erin nodded. "Yes, I know," she said. "And I'll be happy to provide one, if necessary. But surely we can streamline the process? If I could just see the tape from the thirty-first, at eleven twenty-five in the morning, that's all I'd need. Then I'd be out of the way, and there'd be no documentation suggesting there might be any shortfall in your bank's patron-identification procedures." She gave him her best negotiator's smile. For the second time that day, she pictured Carlyle in her head, nodding approval. It was exactly the way he'd have handled something like this.

"Ma'am, I can assure you, we take the security of our customers' accounts extremely seriously," he said, and Erin was satisfied to see him getting a little flustered.

"Then there's nothing to worry about," she said, still smiling pleasantly. "This is just a formality, really. I don't want to make this a bigger deal than it is."

Five minutes later, she was in the security station, watching a tape of the bank from New Year's Eve. The security guard fast-forwarded to eleven twenty and let the tape run. Erin leaned in close. Security-camera footage had come a long way since its early days, but it still tended to be grainy and jumpy, hard to watch. The bank had four active counters that day, and she didn't know at which one the withdrawal had happened.

She didn't see Ronald Whitaker in the line. The minute of the transaction came. People were at each of the counters, none of them resembling the magician.

"Pause it," she said.

The security man obediently froze the frame.

Of the four possible people, one was an overweight, middle-aged woman, two looked like businessmen, and the fourth was a slender, stylishly-dressed woman. The businessmen were dressed in generic suits. One had a mustache and goatee, the other was clean-shaven.

The goatee caught Erin's eye. Facial hair was the thing a witness was most likely to remember about a face. She looked closer. The face looked familiar, but she couldn't say exactly how. It looked like Whitaker, but smaller, thinner. She tried to picture it without the beard and shook her head.

"Rewind a minute," she said. "Then play it again."

She watched the customers approach the counter a second time. This time, she noticed something she'd missed before. The bearded patron let the young woman go first, motioning her with a courteous wave of his hand.

"How long do you retain your footage?" she asked.

"Three months," the man replied.

"Good," she said. "Hang onto it." She was sure the guy in the goatee was the right one. He'd used the woman as a visual distraction. His teller was young and male, and Erin could see the bank employee's eyes follow the attractive woman. The whole thing felt carefully laid out to minimize the chances anyone would pay attention to the bearded man's features.

That didn't do her much good, unless it helped ID the mystery customer. Erin had hoped to find some answers at the bank, but all she had was another question to take back to the precinct with her.

*   *   *

Vic and Webb got back in the midafternoon. They didn't have anything new.

"I did learn one thing," Vic announced.

"What's that?" Erin asked.

"Whitaker's lawyer is a scumbag."

"Really?"

"Yeah. Xavier Morris, Attorney at Law. I ran into him a couple times before. He's an ambulance-chaser, works for a lot of lowlifes. When I was up in the Bronx, a few drug dealers lawyered up with him. Every time I see that weasel, I want to pop him one right in the teeth."

"Everyone's entitled to legal counsel," Webb reminded him.

"I know," Vic said. "But why's it gotta be him? Even two-time losers deserve better defense. I'd rather take my chances with a public defender. At least they've got some principles."

"I guess Whitaker doesn't have a personal lawyer around here," Erin said. "I suppose he didn't say much, with an experienced criminal defense attorney on his elbow?"

"'My client has no comment,'" Webb quoted dryly. "I'm guessing he's worried about a civil suit. Negligence, poor safety standards, something like that."

"I bet the girl's parents sue him," Vic said. "If he's smart, he'll settle out of court. I mean, he tied her to a power saw, for God's sake."

"And she let him," Webb said. "She signed all sorts of personal-injury waivers."

"Lawyers," Vic muttered. But he did seem to be in a marginally better mood in spite of himself. Getting out of the office had done him good.

*   *   *

Erin left work that evening feeling like she was close to something, but not quite there. It was a maddening feeling, like trying to find a missing set of car keys. She just had too much static, too many distractions. Once she could calm down and think clearly, she figured, it would come to her.

Her parking garage had replaced the ceiling lights, but Erin took no chances. She took a second to check the corners, looking for parked cars with people waiting inside. She popped the release on Rolf's compartment before getting out of the car, and had a hand hovering by her sidearm when she climbed out.

Nothing happened, of course. It never did when she was expecting it. Shaking her head wearily, she left the garage and opened the door to her apartment's lobby.

"Evening, love."

Erin just about jumped out of her skin. She had the Glock in her hand and halfway up before she registered the voice, and its familiar accent. Rolf, picking up on her reaction, lunged forward with a snarl.

"Rolf! Bleib!" she snapped. He obediently stopped short.

James Corcoran, leaning calmly against the lobby wall, smiled lazily. He gave no sign of alarm at the fact that she'd nearly put a hole in him, or that a German Shepherd had nearly torn him up. "Rough day at the office, I take it?"

Chapter 15

"Corky." The word was almost a growl.

"The very same," he said cheerfully. "Aren't you going to invite me in? It's perishing cold outside, and downright demeaning to be left standing on the doorstep."

"Depends," Erin said. "What do you want?"

"Just a word, a moment of your time, and perhaps a nip of your excellent Scotch."

"What do I get out of it?"

He grinned. "The pleasure of my company."

"Did Carlyle send you?"

He gave her a wounded look. "I'm here on my own initiative, love. You've grown terribly suspicious. I suspect it's the influence of dealing with so many desperate criminals."

She didn't return the smile. "Look, Corky, you're right. It's been a long day."

"Then the sooner we talk, the sooner I'll be out of your way. I'll be so quick, you'll scarcely know I was inside."

"That line work well with most girls?"

He laughed. "Not quite what I meant, love."

She did crack a smile then. It was so hard to stay angry at Corky. "Okay, come on up. Just for a few minutes. And I'm not offering anything else."

"Perish the thought," he said. "I never ask a lass for anything she's not wanting to give."

She did pour him a glass of Glen D, cracking open the new bottle she'd gotten from the Corner. After all, she needed a drink, and there was no call to be rude. Corky sprawled on Erin's love seat, throwing an arm over its back. Erin sat down in her armchair. Rolf kept a sharp eye on Corky. The K-9's hackles were still slightly raised. He hadn't forgotten that Erin was upset, and wanted Corky to know someone was watching him.

Corky took a sip of whiskey and licked his lips appreciatively. "Ah, that's lovely. Thank you, Erin. You're a right lifesaver. The cold had gone right to my bones."

"How've you been?" Erin asked. She hadn't talked to him in a couple of months.

"As you see me. Still living the good life." He took another drink. "I've my health, my high spirits, and the gifts the good Lord gave me."

"How's business?"

He smiled knowingly. "No complaints."

Corky had good connections with the Teamsters' Union. He was probably involved with about a fair amount the smuggling around Manhattan, and both of them knew it.

"So," Erin said. "You wanted a word. What's the word?"

Corky's smile faded. He leaned forward and set his glass on the coffee table. "I want to talk about Carlyle."

"You said he didn't send you," Erin said sharply.

"He didn't, and he doesn't know I'm here."

"He will," she said. "He's got one of his guys following me around."

"You've met Ian, then," Corky said. "He's a good lad, though a bit serious-minded for my taste. I hope he's not been giving trouble."

"I think he saved me getting my ass kicked," she said.

"That's grand," he said, giving the body part in question a quick but appreciative glance. "And I'm pleased to hear it. But I'm not wanting to talk about him. It's Carlyle, specifically. Have you any idea how the lad feels about you?"

Erin rolled her eyes. "Seriously? You're talking to me about his feelings?"

"Aye." He did look about as serious as she'd ever seen, and she'd seen him hold a bomb's detonator switch open with his fingertips.

"How much do you know?" she demanded.

"I know he's mad about you," Corky said simply.

"That's what he's told you, huh?"

"He's not said a word about it," Corky said. "But remember, I've known the lad all my life. As you know, I've a habit of chasing the lasses. He doesn't. Oh, I've known him to fool about, once or twice, but he doesn't go into relationships lightly."

"Carlyle and I do not have a relationship," she said angrily. "Why does everyone think we do?"

He raised his eyebrows. "Let me ask you something, Erin. If everyone a lad knows tells him he has a drinking problem, but the lad himself says he doesn't, whose word ought we to believe?"

Erin, rendered momentarily speechless with outrage, just glared at him.

Corky, impervious to her glare, picked up his glass and downed the rest of his drink. "I just meant to say, if everyone thinks you've a relationship, perhaps you do, whether it's something you're prepared to admit or not. I've seen my mate, Erin. He's suffering, love. He's downright miserable, pining away. If he were the sort, he'd be writing sad poems and drinking himself to an early grave."

"Okay," Erin said. "So what?"

He looked her straight in the eye. "Our previous history's no secret, love. I'll not deny I was a bit hurt when you turned me down, but not surprised."

"You're a gangster," she said. "I'm a cop."

"Aye, natural enemies," he said. "Like the Catholics and Protestants in the old country. The orange and the green. What you need to understand is, Carlyle isn't like me."

"Meaning what?"

"My mum didn't talk about my da much," Corky said. "Bastard ran off when I was just a wee lad, and I never saw him again. But when she did talk, it was always when I'd done something particularly naughty. She'd say, 'There never was a Corcoran who amounted to anything.' And she was right. Criminals, drunkards, layabouts, the whole sorry lot of us."

Erin watched him and waited. This wasn't what she'd expected him to say.

"I'm a fine lad to share a drink with," he said. "I can show a lass a good time. I know some good jokes, and I'll never betray a friend. But that's about the sum of my good qualities. I'm not the lad you take home to meet your ma."

"And Carlyle is?"

"He's the best man I've ever known," Corky said. "I'm saying that if he loves you, he'll stand by you, no matter what. He'd have died himself, ten times over, to save poor Rose's life, and I've a feeling he'd do the same for you."

He stood up. "Thanks for the drink, Erin, and for hearing me out." He extended his hand. Not knowing quite what to do, she took it. He held on just a moment longer than etiquette suggested. "Think it over, love. Even natural enemies can sometimes find common ground."

"I'll keep that in mind."

He smiled again. "That's grand. I'll see myself out, love. You needn't trouble. And I'll look to see you again, one way or another."

Then he was gone. And Erin realized that her mind wasn't any clearer. If anything, it was much cloudier than before.

* * *

Erin woke up the following morning thinking about the theater. She'd never been a big fan of the stage. Her hardheaded, practical father had passed down his worldview to her. Now she was trying to see into a world built on deception, on pretending to be someone else.

It wasn't all that different from dealing with the criminal underworld, really. She remembered her dad telling her about the old-school Irishmen who'd run organized crime in New York until the Italians had taken over. In particular, Owney Madden, onetime murderer and original owner of the famous Cotton Club, had been friends with the actor Jimmy Cagney. Cagney had modeled his portrayal of gangsters on his buddy. Other gangsters, in turn, had tried to look and act like Cagney. Life imitating art imitating life.

While she took Rolf for their morning run, she kept thinking. Someone in the case was pretending to be something they weren't. Maybe all of them were. Who had been that face in the security camera? It wasn't Louis Miller. He was taller than the goateed man. It wasn't Whitaker himself, though it looked a little like him. If it weren't for the beard, Erin thought, the face would've looked almost feminine.

She abruptly stopped running. Rolf, taken by surprise, took three more strides. Then he realized his partner wasn't with him anymore. He made a tight turn and bounded up on his hind paws, tongue hanging out. They weren't done with their run yet.

"It was a woman," Erin told him. "Wearing a fake beard, dressed as a man. With a fake ID."

Rolf panted and wagged his tail agreeably.

"Okay, okay," she said, starting to run again. Rolf fell in step with her. But she was already thinking ahead.

Chapter 16

"Kathy Grimes," Erin said, hurrying into the office.

"I've heard of her," Vic said. "Isn't she dead, or something?" He was at his desk with a 32-ounce cup of Mountain Dew and a couple of cold Pop Tarts.

"Where's the boss?"

"Dunno. Not in yet." Vic looked up. "You've got something. I can tell."

Erin spun her chair around and sat down. "What's the count on the cash we got from Kathy's hotel room? No, wait, don't tell me. Thirty large, right?"

Vic nodded. "Close enough. This have anything to do with the bank you went to yesterday?"

"Everything," she said. "Kathy was swiping cash from her boss, about ten grand at a time. She dressed up like a guy, put on a fake beard and mustache, and flashed a fake ID at the bank."

"We didn't find a fake ID in her room," Vic pointed out. "Or a beard."

"They worked at a theater," she said. "They've got costumes and dressing rooms."

Vic stood up. "You know what you're looking for?"

"I think so."

"Great. Let's go."

"Before Webb gets here?"

"Screw him," Vic said. "We'll leave him a note. C'mon."

*   *   *

They already had a warrant for the theater. The building was still locked down, to the irritation of its management. New York commercial real estate that wasn't open for business was a big, gaping wound that bled thousands of dollars in lost revenue. Erin hoped their Commercial Crime Insurance policy was paid up to date.

Vic, Erin, and Rolf went in the back with a passkey the theater had provided. They found themselves in the dark backstage corridors. The theater was quiet and deserted.

"This place gives me the creeps," Vic muttered.

"Probably because a girl got sawed in half out front," Erin said.

"No, theaters are just plain spooky," he said. "This is some Phantom of the Opera shit right here."

"Phantom of the Opera," she repeated in a flat voice.

"Hey, I'm just saying, if some guy with acid burns on his face turns up singing, I told you so."

Erin rolled her eyes. "I wouldn't take you for an opera fan."

"I'm not. I used to watch late-night horror movies."

"Whatever." Erin had been looking for a light switch. She found it and flicked it on. The dark hallway was instantly transformed into a plain, ordinary concrete-floored corridor, enlivened by posters of old stage shows. The detectives found Kathy's dressing room easily enough, just a short distance from the stage.

Vic peeled off a pair of disposable gloves from a roll in his back pocket. Erin followed suit. Vic tried the doorknob.

"Unlocked," he said. "Did CSU do this room?"

"I don't think so," Erin said. "This theater's big. They didn't go over the whole place. Just the stage, the front seats, and the backstage area."

Vic opened the door. They entered a small ladies' dressing room, with mirror, lights, and several eye-catching costumes.

He held up a spangly corset with matching bottom. "You think you could bring this off?"

"In your lonely dreams," Erin said. She'd worn swimsuits with more coverage.

Vic grinned. "Okay, what'd she wear to the bank?"

Erin looked at the various outfits. They seemed a little jumbled around. "I think someone's been in here," she said.

"Not our victim?"

"Not a chance," Erin said. "These fabrics are crumpled. Some of them are hung improperly. You gotta be careful with silk. Look, there's a garment bag that's just scrunched up, not covering this dress."

"Erin," Vic said with a smile, "sometimes I forget you're a girl."

"I never forget you're a caveman," she shot back. "Do you even know how to iron a shirt?"

"I use a dry-cleaning service."

"Good. For a second I thought you'd say you just wear things until they're dirty enough to stand up on their own, then throw them out and buy new stuff."

"Hey, that's a good idea."

"Not on our salary, it's not." Erin kept leafing through the clothes. "You're feeling better."

"Not much," he said. "I'll be good once I throw the cuffs on our guy."

"You're lucky Webb didn't give you an insubordination rip."

He grinned again. "I know. Felt good to say it, though."

Erin smiled back. "I feel kinda bad for the poor guy. He has to put up with us."

"Yeah," Vic said. "Our messed-up little dysfunctional family."

"I wonder who was in here," she said, returning her attention to the clothes.

"Probably someone looking for that thirty grand."

She nodded. "Could be the killer." She stooped and picked up a crimson satin glove, elbow-length, that had fallen, or been tossed, to one side. She laid it on the dressing table and went back to her search.

The suit was at the back, hidden in a corner. She reached in and brought it out triumphantly.

"That doesn't belong here," Vic agreed. All the other outfits were performance costumes.

Erin did a quick check of the pockets. "Got something here," she said, pulling out a driver's license. She and Vic took it under the lights for a closer look.

"Ronald Whitaker," Vic read aloud. "I'm not real up on Michigan IDs, but it looks legit to me."

"That's because it is," Erin said, squinting at the piece of plastic. "It's a genuine Michigan license, I'd bet on it. But the photo's been glued on. Look."

"That's some good forgery work," Vic said, holding it up and turning it back and forth. "She must've worked the photo beforehand, got the lines and everything. And check out the shadow image. Damn, how'd she do that?"

"You can see the edges, if you look for them," Erin said. "We could peel this right off. It's not meant to pass a real close check."

"But it's great at arm's length," Vic said. "And I'll bet the license number's accurate. You think our buddy the Great Ronaldo had to have his license replaced recently? Thought it just fell out of his wallet, maybe?"

"I was right," she said. "Kathy was robbing her boss. Thirty thousand in a week."

"He'd have noticed," Vic said.

"That's why she was working fast," Erin said. "She was cleaning out his accounts as quick as she could without provoking a reaction from the bank. I think Kathy was planning to cut loose from Whitaker right here in New York."

"You think Whitaker knew that?" Vic asked.

"I'm starting to wonder," Erin said. "I'm also wondering where Kathy was planning to go." She picked up the discarded red glove she'd found earlier.

"What's that for?" he asked.

"What do you think? The nose knows." She held the glove in front of Rolf's snout. "Rolf, such."

The Shepherd took a deep sniff at the glove. He dipped his head to the floor. Then he went for the door, tail wagging eagerly.

"Erin," Vic said. "If you're trying to track the killer, he's not hanging around here."

"Maybe not," she agreed. "But we might be able to find out where he went." She opened the door. Rolf was off down the hall, pulling steadily at the leash. He was on a good, fresh scent.

He didn't go far. Almost immediately, he stopped in front of another door, whined, and scratched at its base.

"Whitaker's dressing room," Vic said. "Why am I not surprised?"

"Let's have a look," Erin said. She took hold of the doorknob, twisted, and pushed.

The door swung open. The room was dark. She groped for the light switch. Incandescent bulbs flared.

A man was standing in the corner of the room, half-hidden behind a coat-rack.

"Louis Miller?" Erin exclaimed.

He stepped out with a sheepish smile. "Ah, Detective. This is certainly awkward. I can assure you, this isn't what it looks like."

"If I had a dollar for every time someone told me that," Vic said over her shoulder, "I wouldn't have to worry about my dry-cleaning bills."

"I think you better tell me what it is," Erin said. "Before we haul your ass downtown."

Miller gave Erin his very best showman's smile, dazzling white teeth and utterly insincere eyes. "I was simply looking for a few small trinkets, little gifts I'd given Kat. They had sentimental value, though they weren't terribly expensive. I didn't think anyone would mind."

"Sentimental value," Erin repeated. "For the girl you were physically, not romantically, entangled with?"

The grin stayed on his face, looking more artificial by the moment. "I may have understated my attachment to Kat. I really was fond of her."

"That's right," Erin said. "In fact, you were going to run away with her."

The smile faltered. "I beg your pardon?"

"She told her mom. About your plan. That was why she stole Whitaker's money."

"Great disappearing act," Vic added. "The poor bastard's assistant vanishes one day, and then he checks his bank account, and presto! It's gone, too!"

"It would've been a great way to put one over on your rival," Erin said. "And that's one thing you magicians are all about, right? Fooling one another is the best trick of all. So what went wrong? I'm guessing she found out you didn't actually love her."

"I never said I loved her," Miller said. He was definitely looking uncomfortable now. "In fact, I recall saying more or less the opposite to you."

"Yeah, right before you hit on me," she said dryly. "You gotta work on your pickup lines. But you never had any intention of running off with her."

He sighed. "No, I didn't."

"But you told her you would."

He nodded. "You have to understand, Detective, Kat was a born con woman. She spread lies faster than a tabloid newspaper. Do you have any idea how many men she told she loved, only for them to wake up one morning to an empty bank account and a ruined marriage?"

"Yeah, we met one of those guys at a chop shop," Erin said. "He's in jail now, too."

"Grand theft auto," Vic put in.

"That's exactly my point!" Miller said. "She lived by cheating and swindling. Of course I didn't trust her! She didn't trust me, either. We were playing one another!"

"What for?" Erin asked. "Sex?"

"No!" he said. "Well, yes. That was an element of the relationship."

"Money?"

"That, too."

"You were going to con her out of whatever money she got from Whitaker?" Erin shook her head. "That's what you were really looking for here, of course. The thirty thousand she siphoned out of his bank account. You should've gotten your hands on it first."

"Before what?" Miller asked.

"Before you rigged the saw trick," she said.

Miller blinked. "Wait. No, that's not what happened!"

"You saying Kathy didn't get sawed in half?" Vic inquired.

"No! I mean, I didn't kill her!"

"Right," Vic said. "All you did was seduce her, lie to her, conspire to rob her boss, plan to leave her, and then break into a sealed crime scene in order to tamper with evidence and commit burglary. Y'know what, Erin? I don't think I believe this guy when he says he's innocent. Any idea why?"

"Because he's a lying piece of shit," she said.

"My thoughts exactly," Vic said. He pulled out his handcuffs. "And I was right. I'm already feeling a whole lot better."

"Wait," Miller said. "You can't be serious."

"You spend a lot of time with people who lie for a living," Erin said. "So believe me when I say I'm dead serious. Louis Miller, you're under arrest for conspiracy to commit grand larceny, and for the murder of Kathy Grimes. You have the right to remain silent. Anything you say can and will be used against you in a court of law. You have the right to an attorney. If you cannot afford an attorney, one will be assigned to you by the court. Do you understand these rights?"

"I..." he started. Then he shrugged resignedly. "Yes, I understand. But are you sure you want to do this, Detectives?"

"I'm pretty sure I do," Vic said, brandishing the cuffs. "Turn around and place your hands behind your back."

A thin smile came back to Miller's face. "Are you watching closely?" he asked.

Vic snapped the cuffs closed. "Yeah. I am."

"You want to take him out to the car?" Erin asked.

"Sure," Vic said. "What're you doing?"

"I just want to take another quick look around, see if we missed anything else."

"Okay," he said. "I'll be outside if you need me."

Chapter 17

Erin and Rolf were left alone in the theater. She scratched the K-9 behind the ears. "Good boy," she said. He'd done a great job tracking Miller, and he was still enjoying his payoff. Rolf was busily gnawing his chew-toy, not a care in the world.

While the dog enjoyed his reward, she considered the situation. She should have felt good about the case; they had their suspect in custody, everything seemed to fit together. But she was uneasy. Something was missing.

"Miller wanted the money," she said to Rolf. "Kathy had it hidden in her hotel room. But Miller didn't know that. So he came in and ransacked the costume room. But why didn't he look for the money back when he sabotaged the machine?"

Rolf wagged his tail agreeably, showing he was listening, but kept his attention focused on the rubber ball. As far as he was concerned, the ball was the very best thing in the world.

"If he had backstage access, why take the risk of showing up twice?" she went on. "And if he didn't find the money, why kill Kathy? Wouldn't it be better to keep her alive, pretend to run off with her, and get the cash later?"

She pressed a hand to her forehead and tried to think. She could really use a drink. It would steady her out, calm her down.

"No," she said, suddenly a little scared. Was this really what she was coming down to? A woman who needed a drink just to get through the day? Was she turning into an alcoholic?

Rolf cocked his head at her. His jaws kept working the ball.

She couldn't help smiling at the ridiculous picture of her badass K-9 chomping a rubber ball like a two-month pup. "Gonna do better, partner," she said. "Have to."

Erin glanced into the room where they'd busted Miller. Whitaker's dressing room. Why'd he been hanging out there? No way would Kathy have stashed the cash in her boss's room.

"He had another reason for being here," she said slowly, nodding to herself. "It wasn't just about the money. He was checking up on his rival. Maybe looking for some trade secrets. These guys are always trying to put one over on each other. Whitaker would do the same thing to him. Hell, they booked theaters across the street from each other."

The rivalry was the important thing. Each magician was trying to beat the other. But what had Whitaker done to Miller? Nothing that Erin knew of. But that was the thing about magic. What you saw was only half of what was going on.

"Whitaker wins," Erin said. That was the truth. His rival was out of the way, he gained a lot of press. He lost an assistant, but so what? The world was full of wannabe-starlets who'd love to put on a rhinestone-studded bikini and prance around the stage. For some of them, the danger would just be an added thrill. Besides, Kathy had been robbing him. She was no great loss, in the end. But that line of thinking only made sense if...

"Holy shit," she said. "What if that's the magic trick? That there's no trick at all? What if what happened on stage was exactly what it looked like?"

Excitement rushed through her in a way it hadn't during this whole damn sordid mess of a case. She wanted to take another look on stage, just to remind herself. But she was already sure.

"Rolf, komm!" she ordered.

He obediently got to his feet and deposited his beloved toy in her hand. The now-slimy ball went into her jacket pocket. Then they went to look at the murder scene one more time.

*   *   *

They approached the stage from behind, through the service hallways. Erin saw various paraphernalia of the show laid out, ready for use. To a detective, it was a ghastly set of props. Swords, throwing knives, shackles, a drowning tank. It was practically a murder buffet. She wondered how they all could've been so blind.

The curtains were closed. The evidence techs had drawn them down to make sure they could catalog any stray blood-spatter that might have gotten lost in the heavy velvet folds. Erin and Rolf walked toward the curtains. Rolf sniffed the stage with interest. The smell of blood and death was fainter than it had been, but if Erin could still smell it, she knew it would be filling the dog's nostrils.

She froze. Voices were coming through the curtain. A man and a woman.

"...feels kind of funny being here," the woman said. "Spooky. It gives me the creeps, a little."

"That's part of the ambience," said the man, whose voice was familiar. "Remember, with a magic show, the danger is part of the point. It's like a roller-coaster. Haven't you ever screamed during a scary movie?"

The woman giggled. "Yeah."

"It's the same here. We'll put you in black. You'll be a spirit guide, a medium. Did you know, stage magic and séances have been linked for a hundred years? Harry Houdini was a spiritualist. You'd be fantastic in black, maybe with some silver thread laced through. You've got a great complexion for the spotlight, that pale skin, almost translucent."

"Oh, stop it," the woman said, but Erin could hear she didn't really mean it. "Mr. Whitaker—"

"Please, call me Ron. If we're going to be working together, we need to be on a first-name basis."

Erin had heard enough. She was pissed off now. The nerve of this guy. She went quickly to the curtain and stepped through.

"I hope I'm not interrupting something," she said with false cheeriness.

Ronald Whitaker stood just a few feet in front of her, facing a young woman. The woman was dark-haired and very pretty. Whitaker had his hand on her arm and was standing very close to her. When he heard Erin's voice, he let go of the girl and stepped back reflexively.

"Detective!" he exclaimed. "This is a surprise."

"I'll bet," she said. "If it wasn't, I don't think you'd be holding a job interview at an active crime scene. With the blood of her predecessor on the stage." She cocked her head toward the shockingly large stain that discolored the stage and front few rows of seats.

"Who're you?" the girl asked.

"Detective O'Reilly," Erin said. "NYPD Major Crimes. I'm investigating the murder of Kathy Grimes. Some people called her Kat. She wasn't what you'd call a good girl. Always in trouble with the law, with a bunch of guys on her trail who'd have loved to hurt her. But she was always able to keep one step ahead of them. She cheated and conned every guy she ever met, but she was so pretty and charming, she got away with it.

"Until she made a fatal mistake. She made an offer to her boss's rival. She'd take the boss's money and his secrets, and they'd run off to live happily ever after as a successful stage couple."

Erin paused. "I don't know which betrayal hurt the most. Was it the money, the magic, or the sex?"

Whitaker's brow wrinkled. "I don't know what you're talking about, Detective."

"It's a funny thing," she said. "I've talked to a lot of perps over the years. Innocent people never say they don't know what I'm talking about. Not once. They ask what I mean. Because they don't know. The guilty ones, they know just fine.

"I expect you found out your bank balance was running a little low," she continued. "Either that or you were already suspicious of Kathy. Were you sleeping with her, too?"

"That's none of your business," he said. "The relationships of two consenting adults aren't within the NYPD's purview."

Erin shook her head, ignoring his words. "You couldn't resist, though. Simple revenge wasn't good enough for you. You had to hurt Kathy, had to do something really awful to her. And public. You wanted us to find out. You know that lots of perps want to get caught? They want to tell their story. To be understood. Ron, I know what Kathy did to you. She betrayed you completely. She treated you like dirt. After everything you did for her, too."

"She'd be shaking her ass on stage for dollar bills stuffed in her G-string without me," Whitaker snapped, and Erin was stunned by the sudden change in him. "All that girl knew how to do was screw men, one way or another. Oh, she was good at it. That girl was sex on two legs. If you'd ever seen her... man. She was something else. I pulled her out of Detroit. You know what that town is like? I gave her a future, I gave her an audience! But she couldn't resist cheating, at everything she ever did."

Erin nodded. She had a hand resting on the butt of her Glock now, just in case. She had no idea whether he was armed, and a cop always assumed the worst. "I think it was especially clever how you pinned it on Miller," she said. "Was that the plan all along, or just a fringe benefit?"

Whitaker smiled at her, one of the most chilling smiles she'd ever seen. She hadn't truly pegged him for a psychopath until that moment. "A good magician never reveals all his secrets," he said.

"Ron?" the girl asked hesitantly. Both Erin and Whitaker had been ignoring her. They glanced her way now. "What's she saying, Ron?"

"He killed Kathy Grimes," Erin said. "Sawed her in half, in front of hundreds of people. You might want to reconsider your employment prospects."

"She betrayed me!" Whitaker snapped. "She stole thirty thousand dollars! Do you have any idea how hard it is to get that kind of money? And she was fucking that worthless, smarmy, no-talent jackass Miller! The Amazing Lucien! It's amazing he can walk across the stage without falling over. Of course he was trying to steal my tricks! He stole everything! He never worked for anything in his life. Do you have any idea how much work, how much planning went into my act? The timing? The showmanship of it? And she was going to make me look like an idiot. She was laughing at me the whole time. All of them were. I might as well have been wearing clown makeup out there, with white face-paint and a red nose. She wanted to hurt me."

"So you hurt her," Erin said. "Makes sense."

"I loved her! This is her fault, not mine! She made me do it. That girl would drive anyone crazy!"

"Okay," she said. "I think that'll do it. Ronald Whitaker, you're under arrest for the murder of Kathy Grimes. You have the right to remain—"

Whitaker was fast. One moment he was standing there, shouting. The next, he was behind the girl. Something bright and shiny dropped out of his sleeve into his hand, and he was suddenly pressing a sharp-looking knife against her throat.

Erin snatched out her Glock. "Drop it!" she shouted. "Put your hands in the air! I'll shoot you if I have to!" Rolf bristled and growled, waiting for his takedown command.

"Put the gun down, Detective. You wouldn't want me to get nervous and slip." Whitaker was moving to the side, dragging the terrified young woman with him. Erin turned, tracking him, aiming at his head. She couldn't chance a shot. If she put a finger inside the trigger guard, he could slit the girl's throat before she could fire. Siccing Rolf on him wasn't the answer either. The dog was fast, but not fast enough. But there was no way she was letting him walk out of the theater with a hostage.

"Give it up, Whitaker," she said. "There's only two ways this ends. Either you leave in handcuffs, or in a body bag. It's your choice."

He smiled again, and said the same thing Miller had said not ten minutes before. "Are you watching closely, Detective?"

She was, but in spite of what she and Miller had discussed, she was watching the wrong hand, the knife hand. Whitaker's left hand flexed. A small sphere dropped to the stage. It struck with a bright flash and a puff of smoke, like an old camera flashbulb. There was a bang like a gunshot.

The girl stumbled toward Erin, out of the smoke cloud.

"Get behind me!" Erin ordered. She kept her pistol leveled.

The smoke was slow to dissipate. As it drifted toward the ceiling, Erin saw only an empty stage.

Ronald Whitaker was gone.

Chapter 18

"You've gotta be shitting me," Erin said aloud.

"Help," the girl said. She clutched at Erin's arm.

Erin pulled free of her. This was no time to get tangled up with a civilian. "How'd you get in?" she snapped.

"I... I don't..."

"Front door? Back? Talk to me!"

"Side..."

"Can you get out the same way?"

"I... I think so..."

"Go. Now! Find another officer, tell them what happened."

Erin's words had the desired effect. A little focus came back into the girl's eyes. She turned and left the auditorium in a stumbling run, hobbled by her high heels.

Erin grabbed her phone and speed-dialed Vic.

"Miss me?" he said lazily.

"Get your ass in here! Whitaker's here! He killed Kathy!"

"On my way," Vic said, coming instantly alert. "Where are you?"

"Center stage." Erin kept turning, trying to cover every exit. "He pulled a vanishing act. Could be anywhere. Rolf! Such!"

The Shepherd cocked his head, and Erin could see him trying to figure out which person he was supposed to follow. She pointed where Whitaker had been standing. The dog walked to the spot she'd indicated, ducked his head, sniffed, and began scratching at the boards of the stage.

"No," she said. "I need to know where he went!"

Rolf kept scratching. He whined.

Then she saw it, the faint outline of a trap door. "Son of a bitch," she murmured. "Good boy! Zei brav!"

The K-9 wagged his tail and kept scratching. Erin ran to the door and looked for a button, a handle, anything. She couldn't see any way of opening it. Lifting a foot, she stomped as hard as she could. The boards held, but the door rattled and gave a little. She stomped again. Wood creaked and cracked.

"Rolf! Hier!" she ordered.

He obediently returned to her side.

She briefly considered waiting for Vic. But Whitaker knew the ground better than she did, and already had a head start. Every wasted second made it more likely he'd be able to escape the theater altogether.

"Well, here goes," she muttered and jumped on the trapdoor as with all her weight.

The latch gave way. She dropped straight down in a shower of splinters. Erin fell no more than eight or nine feet. She dimly saw some sort of pad, like a wrestling mat, rush up to meet her. She tried to bend her knees to take the impact, but went down heavily on her hip. She kept her grip on her gun, rolled to the side, and came up to one knee, ignoring the flare of pain in her leg.

Rolf barked twice, sharply, looking down at his partner.

Erin got to her feet and quickly scanned the space under the stage. Whitaker was nowhere in sight. The only illumination was the red-glowing letters of an exit sign.

"Rolf! Hupf!" she called, giving him his "jump" command.

He didn't hesitate. She heard the thump of his landing. Then he was there beside her, none the worse for wear.

"Such!" she told him again. He was off toward the exit. Erin ran after him, catching up at the door. He scratched at the base of it and gave his signal whine.

Erin hit the door's locking bar at full tilt and launched herself into a basement hallway. She plunged into a cloud of thick, dark smoke that smelled like gunpowder. Whitaker apparently hadn't run out of tricks yet. As she waved a hand in front of her face, she felt Rolf push past her thigh. He vanished into the smoke. She followed.

It was nearly pitch-black. There were a few faint emergency lights, but the smoke blotted them out. Erin had left her flashlight in the car. She promised herself never to make that mistake again. Up ahead, she heard Rolf bark. Then came a sound that buried her confusion and caution in an avalanche of pure rage. It was the distinctive rapid-fire click-click-click of a Taser, accompanied by her K-9 yelping in pain.

Erin ran. She came out of the smoke cloud at a T-junction. Rolf was lying on the floor, legs kicking in helpless spasms. It was too dark to see the Taser wires, so she couldn't tell where the darts had come from. She had to guess, left or right. She pivoted right, Glock leveled.

Ronald Whitaker stood in the middle of the hallway, a Taser pistol in one hand, the blade of his knife gleaming in the other. In the red emergency lights, the weapon looked bloody. He cocked his arm back in a wind-up.

"Drop it!" she shouted.

He just smiled. His hand was poised.

Erin fired twice, center mass. Whitaker shattered. One moment he was there, the next his image fell apart in sparkling shards.

It was a mirror, Erin realized, cleverly angled so she hadn't noticed her own reflection. Which meant Whitaker was behind her. She started to turn, twisting sideways.

The knife tumbled end-over-end. If she hadn't been quick, it would have buried itself squarely between her shoulder blades. She felt a sudden, deep, sickening pain in her arm, just above the elbow. The Glock dropped out of her hand and spun across the floor with the momentum of her turn.

Whitaker put out a foot and stopped the skittering pistol under his toe. He dropped the Taser carelessly to one side and stooped to pick up Erin's gun. He was still smiling.

"Presto," he said.

Erin gritted her teeth, ignoring the pain, ignoring the knife that still jutted from her arm. She went down to a crouch, going for her backup ankle gun, knowing she didn't have time to draw it.

"That's all, folks," Whitaker said.

Tasers were one of the many things portrayed inaccurately in the movies. On screen, when someone took a jolt of the happy juice, they went down unconscious. In reality, Tasers incapacitated their victims by locking up muscles, overriding the brain's electrical impulses with their own high-voltage shock. But they only worked as long as the current was flowing. Rolf had ridden the lightning, but the Taser's timer had run out and now his muscles worked just fine. Pain didn't stop the K-9; it just made him mad.

The dog twisted his body, coming up off the floor with astonishing speed. Whitaker's mouth dropped open. Before he could recover, Rolf sprang at him and clamped his jaws on the magician's forearm. When his partner had been attacked, he didn't need anyone to tell him what to do.

Whitaker didn't even get a shot off. The dog's jaws flexed, bone cracked, and Erin's Glock hit the floor for the second time.

The magician followed it down, dragged to the ground by ninety pounds of pissed-off K-9.

Erin came up with her backup revolver in her left hand. She hurried to the fallen man and snatched up her sidearm. "Don't move," she said through clenched teeth. "You fight him, it only gets worse."

"Erin! Erin!"

"Down here, Vic!" she yelled. "Under the stage, down the hallway!"

A flashlight beam showed through the smoke-bomb's murk. It was followed in short order by Vic, flashlight in one hand, pistol in the other. The big Russian took in the scene. Erin was standing over her dog and her prisoner, guns in both hands, blood running down her arm.

He whistled. "Damn, girl. How come you gotta have all the fun without me?"

"Shut up and cover this asshole," she growled, holstering her guns and taking out her cuffs. "As I was saying, Ronald Whitaker, you're under arrest. You have the right to remain silent..."

*   *   *

Once they had the cuffs on Whitaker, Erin yanked the Taser needles out of Rolf. The dog was apparently uninjured, but he kept bristling and growling, giving Whitaker a very unfriendly stare. Only then did Erin let Vic take a look at her arm.

"You're fine," he announced after a quick inspection. "It went in the bicep, clean entry. The artery's not hit, and neither is the bone. We'd better leave it in until we get a first-aid kit. It'll bleed some, and you'll want to get it stitched up, but it'll just leave a scar."

"And chicks dig scars, right?" she said.

"Damn right," he said. "Hey, you got stabbed in a knife fight. Not everyone can say that."

"I'd hardly call it a knife fight," Whitaker said.

"Shut up," Vic said. "You're just lucky my partner's more forgiving than I am. I oughta take this knife out of her and shove it right up your magic ass."

"I'll be filing suit against the department, of course," Whitaker went on. "Excessive force. A magician's hands are his greatest asset. Your animal broke my arm. This is a career-affecting injury. When my lawyer hears—"

"When your lawyer hears what went down," Vic said with a grim smile, "he's just gonna have two words for you. The first one is 'plea,' the second is 'bargain.' Morris is a weasel, but he's a smart weasel. I'd listen to him."

"You've got a class A misdemeanor for zapping my dog," Erin said. "Plus a class B violent felony for knifing me. That's on top of the murder charge. You ever want to see the street again, I agree with Vic." She turned to the other detective. "Let's get the hell out of here."

They followed the Exit signs to a back stairway, which eventually led them to the service door by which they'd entered the theater. Vic held on to Whitaker, letting Erin concentrate on her injury and her dog. They stepped outside and started toward Erin's Charger, which was where they'd left it in the alley.

"Hey, Vic?" Erin asked as they got closer. "What'd you do with Miller?"

"He's in the back," Vic said.

She squinted at the tinted glass. "No, he's not."

"Yeah, he is," Vic said. "I left the cuffs on him and everything."

Erin opened the back door of her car and wordlessly indicated an empty vehicle.

Vic stood there like he'd taken a baseball bat to the face. He blinked a couple of times. "He's not here," he finally said.

Erin felt a slightly hysterical smile spread across her face. "Tell me again, Vic, how you left a magician all alone, handcuffed, in a locked car?"

"Son of a bitch," he said, shaking his head ruefully. "Son of a goddamn bitch. I'm never gonna live this one down, am I?"

"Not a chance," she said. "Better call it in. We've got one in custody, and another running. We'll put out a BOLO. I don't care if he's a magician, I don't think he'll get far. Now, if you don't mind, I'd like to get this knife out of my arm."

Chapter 19

"O'Reilly. Neshenko. Something you want to share with me?" Webb asked.

"Sorry, sir," Erin said. "We got sidetracked."

"But we got our guy," Vic said.

"Really? Who?"

"Whitaker," Vic said. "Turns out, he sawed his assistant in half."

"We knew that already," Webb said. "Did you find out who monkeyed with his equipment?"

"He did it himself," Erin said. "He wanted to make it look like someone else sabotaged it. He hoped we'd blame Miller."

"Which we did," Vic said. "For about, oh, five minutes."

"I got a confession out of Whitaker," Erin said. "Plus, he tased my dog. And stabbed me."

Webb stood up suddenly. "You hurt? Where?"

"It's not bad." She flexed her right arm with more enthusiasm than she really wanted to. Pain pulsed through her bicep. She tried to suppress a wince. "We swung by Urgent Care on the way back to the precinct. I got it stitched up. I'll be fine."

"Jesus." Webb sat down again. "You didn't shoot Whitaker, did you?"

"No, but Rolf bit him," she said. "Whitaker needed some first aid, too. But he'll be okay to stand trial."

"Your dog got tased, and then bit him anyway?"

"He's a badass, sir," Erin said.

Rolf gave Webb a look as if to say he was, indeed, a badass.

"And you got stabbed, but successfully arrested him?" Webb went on.

"Yes, sir," Erin said.

"She's a badass, too," Vic said.

"Where were you while all this was going down?"

"I was watching our other prisoner."

"Who is...?"

"Louis Miller," Erin said.

"But he didn't kill Grimes."

"No," she confirmed.

"So you turned him loose?"

Erin glanced at Vic. "Not exactly," she said. "He was involved with a conspiracy to steal thirty thousand dollars. Plus he broke into a crime scene."

"Okay," Webb said. "Where's he now?"

Erin and Vic shared another glance.

"What?" Webb asked.

"I called Vic for backup," Erin said. "He left Miller cuffed in my Charger. It turns out, leaving an escape artist by himself wasn't a good way to keep him in custody."

Webb actually cracked a smile. "So he's in the wind?"

"We already put out a BOLO," she said.

"And where's Whitaker? You didn't lose him, too, did you?"

"No," she said. "He's in Interrogation Room One, waiting for his lawyer."

"How solid is the evidence?" Webb asked.

"Most of it is fairly circumstantial," she admitted. "But he assaulted my dog and tried to kill me. And he did confess in front of a civilian."

"Tell me you got her statement," Webb said.

"No, but she ran straight to the nearest squad car," Vic said, glad to give his commanding officer some good news. "Told them a crazy magician had held her at knife-point and was fighting with a cop. We'll have her in shortly."

Webb smiled more broadly. "It's always a pleasant surprise when civvies do the right thing," he said. "So we've got Whitaker on assaulting her, too?"

"He took her hostage and held a knife to her throat," Erin confirmed.

"This guy's toast," Vic said.

"Not even lunchtime yet," Webb said. "What are we going to do with the rest of the day?"

"Well, sir..." Erin began.

"That was rhetorical, O'Reilly," he interrupted. "You're going to do paperwork. You can start with the 61s, then the DD-5s, then the arrest reports, and... Get back here, Neshenko! Your name needs to be on the forms, too."

Vic had been unsuccessfully attempting to sidle out of the Major Crimes office. He shuffled back to his desk and sat down with a sigh.

"Sir, I have one other thing to take care of," Erin said.

"What's that?" Webb asked.

"Loose end from the Bucklington case."

"Auto Crimes has him."

"It's just one thing to run down."

"Can you do it from this office?"

"No," she admitted. "I have to go up to the Bronx."

"Then you can do it after you've finished your paperwork," Webb said relentlessly. "God, I feel like a substitute teacher today."

Vic glanced up. "It's okay, Erin," he said. "Just tell him your dog ate your arrest reports."

*   *   *

Erin was already kicking herself as she drove up to the Bronx in the late afternoon. She should've taken care of this business already. She'd just been too distracted, too upset, not herself.

She'd swung by home to drop off Rolf; for this job, she needed the back of her car empty.

The 49th Precinct in the Bronx was an intimidating stack of bricks, larger and in better repair than Erin's own Eightball. Erin thought it looked almost like a military bunker, or maybe a prison.

The desk sergeant directed her to the Auto Crimes division, where she found Detective Curtiss, a stocky, balding man in a suit a little too small for him. He gave her half a glance.

"Okay, be right with you, ma'am," he said. He returned his attention to his computer screen.

Erin raised her eyebrows and waited.

"All right," he said without looking up. "Make and model?"

"Excuse me?"

He sighed. "Your car, lady. What's the make and model?"

"Sir, my name's Erin O'Reilly," she said. "I'm with NYPD Major Crimes, Detective Second Grade. If you're not too busy, there's something I'd like your help with."

That got his attention. Curtiss pushed his chair back from his desk. "Sorry, Detective," he said, standing up and offering his hand. "This neighborhood, a white woman walks into Auto Crimes out of uniform, I just assumed—"

"Forget about it," she said, shaking hands. "I drive a Charger, in case you're wondering."

He laughed. "Not stolen, I hope."

"Nope. Department-issue."

"What can I do for you, Detective?"

"We sent you a guy, Hugo Bucklington. Grand Theft Auto. A kid, too, name of Devon James."

"Right," Curtiss said. "Thanks for that. They've been running a chop shop for a while, cutting up a lot of hot wheels." He laughed again. "He's cooperating nicely. We're looking to bust up several street crews with what he's giving us. He plays his cards right, he hits the street again in six months and we nail half a dozen professional car thieves."

"Great," Erin said. "I was actually wondering about his dog."

"His what?"

"His junkyard dog. Big, black, furry, answers to Ripper when he feels like it?"

"Oh, yeah," Curtiss said. "That. You sure it's a dog?"

"Pretty sure. Where is he?"

Curtiss shrugged. "We handed it off to a local shelter. The kid, Devon, told us his brother would take him, but the brother ran off when a uniform went looking for him. Turns out the brother had warrants on him, too."

"Which shelter?" Erin asked.

Curtiss scribbled the address on a Post-it and handed it to her.

"Thanks," she said, turning to go.

"Detective," he called.

She paused. "What?"

"You drove all the way up from, where, Precinct 8?"

"Yeah."

"For a dog?"

"Yeah."

"What's so important about it?"

Erin smiled thinly. "I'm a K-9 cop, Detective."

*   *   *

When she got to the animal shelter, she immediately knew she should have gotten there faster. It was a filthy, noisy dump of a place. Litter was strewn carelessly around an overflowing trash can out front. The whole area stank of dog shit and urine. Dogs barked on all sides, their voices overlapping one another.

Erin wouldn't have put hardened murderers in a place like that. Dog lover that she was, it was all she could do to keep herself under control and walk in the front door.

"We're just about to close," said the tired-looking woman at the front desk.

"This won't take long," Erin said. "I'm looking for Ripper."

"Ripper?"

"Black, shaggy mixed-breed, dropped off by the police."

"Oh, yeah, I remember him," the woman said. "Nasty piece of work. Tried to bite our handler."

Erin's heart skipped a beat. "What happened to him?"

"He's fine. Dog missed him."

"Not the handler," she said through gritted teeth. "The dog."

"Oh, right. They put him down."

"They what?" Erin's fists were clenched at her sides.

The woman gave her a look of weary contempt. "Save it, sister. This place holds a hundred and fifty animals. We've got a budget that lets us take good care of maybe a hundred. Last week, we had two hundred to keep track of. We'll place maybe thirty of those. The rest get put down. A junkyard dog with a biting problem? He wouldn't have a chance of getting adopted."

"When did it happen?"

The woman shrugged. "They brought him in last night, after close. The vet just came in about a half hour ago. There's a long list to work through. It'll be any minute."

"Where is he now?" Erin snapped.

"Look, sister, I don't know who you think you are, but you can't—"

Erin put her shield in the woman's face. "NYPD," she interrupted. "Now where's the vet?"

"Down the back hallway, take the last left."

Erin was gone, running in the direction the woman indicated. She passed a line of dog pens. The dogs, excited by her motion, jumped up and put their paws on the chain-link fencing, barking even more furiously than before. She ignored them, making for the door at the end of the hall.

She burst in on a veterinarian, a dog handler, and Ripper. They had him up on the table. He was lying quietly, and the vet was poised with a syringe. The dog wasn't moving, and for a moment she thought she was too late. Then she saw the syringe was still full.

"Stop!" she shouted.

"Who are you?" the handler demanded.

"You can't just come in here," the vet said. "We're in the middle of a delicate operation."

"Yeah, I know," she said. "You're killing that dog."

"I'm doing the most humane thing possible, under the circumstances," the vet said. "He's been sedated, so he won't feel anything. Now I'm just going to inject him, and he'll go quietly, in his sleep."

"That's not gonna happen," Erin said.

"This animal is vicious," the handler said. "He can't be adopted."

"And your shelter is overcrowded," she said. "I know. So I'll take him off your hands."

"You're not listening, ma'am," the handler said. "This is a liability issue. If you take him, and he bites you, we could get sued."

"I'm with the NYPD K-9 unit," she said. "So yeah, I know all about lawyers. But I don't like them very much. Just give me the damn dog and I'll get out of your hair."

"There's an adoption fee—" the handler started.

That was when Erin lost her temper. "You're five seconds from killing this dog, and now you want to charge me for him?" she snapped. "Here." She reached into her pocket, pulled out her wallet, grabbed the first bill she found in it, and slapped it down on the table next to Ripper's sleeping body. It was a twenty. "That do you? You happy?"

Both people stared at her. Neither said anything.

Erin scooped up the dog in her arms. His dead weight made a large, smelly armful, but she didn't ask for help. She turned and started walking out the door.

"Why this one?" the vet asked. "Ma'am, I have to put down dozens of dogs. You can't take all of them."

"If I let myself think that way," she said, "I'd never get out of bed in the morning."

She put Ripper in the K-9 compartment in the back of her car. So far, she'd been going on instinct and emotion. Now she needed a plan. She thought for a minute, then pulled out her phone.

"Hey, Shelley?"

"Erin!" Michelle said. "Did you get your man?"

"Yeah, we made an arrest."

"That's not what I meant. I was talking about the guy you've been seeing."

"Oh. No, I'm not seeing anyone."

"Why not?"

"Shelley, that's not why I'm calling."

"I know. But it's on your mind."

"Can we talk about this later?"

"When?"

Erin closed her eyes. "Just later, okay? Right now I've got a junkyard dog passed out in the back of my squad car."

"Is that code for something?"

"No, it's an actual dog. And he doesn't smell too good. I'm already gonna have to hose out the back of the car before I put Rolf back in it."

"Erin, are you sidelining as a dogcatcher now?"

"No." Erin explained the situation with Ripper. "He doesn't have anywhere to go," she finished. "The vet was about to shoot him up with poison when I got there. I had to get him out of there."

"Is he really a sweet dog at heart?"

"No more than any other dog," Erin said. "He's kind of a mean, ugly son of a bitch, when you get down to it. But that doesn't rate a death sentence. He needs some retraining, and a strong guiding hand, but he could be a good enough dog. If you know a decent no-kill shelter we could put him at while I figure something out..."

"Of course," Michelle said. "Anna's really been on me about that puppy, so I've started doing some research. Just in case. There's a place just up the street. I'll give them a call. Come on down."

"Yeah, I remembered what you said at lunch about getting a dog. That's why I called you. Thanks."

"Don't mention it. You can pay me back."

Erin rolled her eyes. "I bet I can guess how."

"All I want is information, sis."

"Okay, okay. I'll tell you, once we get Ripper taken care of."

"That's his name? For real?"

"I'm afraid so."

"We'll tell the shelter folks he's named Roger. How's that sound?"

"Good idea, Shelley."

Erin hung up and shot Ripper a look. He was lying on his side, his tongue hanging half out of his mouth. He was giving off an indescribable odor.

"You better be worth it, big guy," she said.

Chapter 20

"That," Michelle said, "was the ugliest dog I've ever seen in my life."

Erin smiled. They were at a bistro just down the street from Ripper's new temporary home, after grabbing a quick dinner. Michelle had a soy mocha latte in front of her. Erin had a basic cup of coffee, cream, no sugar. "I dunno," she said. "He kind of grows on you."

"What kind of dog is he, anyway?" Michelle asked.

"Beats me. Something big and shaggy, crossed with a Doberman, I guess. Maybe part grizzly bear or wolverine."

Michelle laughed. "I hope he finds a good home, with someone who appreciates his... unique qualities."

"He's not a bad dog," Erin said quietly. "There's no such thing."

"You like dogs better than people, don't you."

"On average? Yeah."

"Why'd you save this one?"

Erin stared into her coffee cup. "I don't know."

"Yes you do."

"Is this an interrogation, Shelley?"

Michelle smiled. "If you cooperate now, we'll go easy on you."

"I've heard that before," Erin said. "Hell, I've said it before."

"So why'd you go out of your way for one ugly mutt?"

"Maybe it's that he was only there because I arrested his owner," she said. "So that made it my fault, a little. Maybe it's that he wagged his tail when I left him at the junkyard. I think I saw the good boy inside, trying to get out in spite of everything."

Michelle nodded. "Sean tells me doctors sometimes develop a bit of a God complex, choosing who lives and who dies. He says it's dangerous, especially in the ER. Are police officers like that, too?"

Erin shrugged. "I guess we're a lot like docs. We see all the worst people can do to each other, and we try to straighten out what we can. I can't save everyone, sure. But I could save Ripper... Roger, I mean. And just because I couldn't save all the other dogs didn't mean I had an excuse to let this one die. I don't think that makes me God."

"No, I guess not," Michelle said. "But you think Roger's got a chance?"

"As good as a lot of dogs."

"How about your mystery man?"

"What?"

"Does he have a chance? With you?"

Erin glared at her. "You just don't give up."

"Nope," Michelle said, unrepentant. "Erin, you're not good at being mysterious. What's the deal with this guy? Are you ashamed of him?"

"Shelley, I'm not seeing him. It's... it's complicated."

"Oh!" she exclaimed. "He's married! You naughty girl!"

"No!"

Michelle frowned. "Okay, so... he's somebody famous. A celebrity."

"No."

"Erin, don't make me guess. I've got a long list of possibilities, and I swear, I'll go through every one of them."

Erin sighed. "Okay, Shelley, here's the thing. If any of this gets out at work, I could get in trouble. I'm serious."

Michelle held up one hand. "I swear, I won't tell a single soul."

Erin believed her. Michelle loved to hear about people, but she wasn't big on gossiping to others. If she swore herself to secrecy, she meant it.

"I met this guy through work, okay?" Erin said, not quite sure how to begin.

"Another officer?"

"No."

"Oh, gosh," Michelle said. "Is he a family member of a victim? Did his wife get murdered?"

"Shelley! No!" Erin exclaimed. Then she paused. "Well, actually, yeah, his wife did get murdered. But that was years ago, long before I met him."

"So, how did you meet?"

"He was a suspect, if you gotta know."

Michelle's eyes got wide. "Really?"

Erin nodded. "He didn't do it. The thing we were looking at, I mean. The problem is, he's done some other stuff."

"Erin. You're in love with a criminal?"

"I didn't say that!" she snapped.

"Well?" Michelle asked. "Are you, though?"

"I don't know," Erin said. "But I'm pretty sure he's in love with me."

"Is he a basically good guy, who's done some bad things? Or is he bad right through?"

"He's..." Erin paused.

"Complicated?" Michelle prompted.

"Yeah." She sighed again. "It wasn't supposed to go like this. He helped out with a couple of things, I helped him a little, we became friends... God, what was I thinking? He's a gangster, Shelley! I may have to arrest him someday!"

"So why are you even thinking about it?"

"Because he's... him. He talks to me like no one else does. He's polite, he's smart, he respects me. I... I trust him, in spite of everything."

"Is he hot?"

"Shelley!"

"It's a valid question," Michelle said. "Have the two of you... you know..."

"Something happened after the thing at the Civic Center," Erin said. "Without his help, we might not have been in time to stop that bomb going off. He probably saved a couple hundred lives. Including mine. I went by his place afterwards, we talked, and then..."

"And then...?" Michelle echoed.

"You've got no shame at all," Erin said. "You watch a lot of reality TV, don't you?"

"All the time," Michelle said cheerfully. "I'm a housewife, Erin. I've got no life of my own, so I have to take it where I find it."

"He kissed me."

"You kiss him back?"

"Yeah."

"How was it?"

"It was good," Erin admitted. "Until I remembered what was going on and got myself the hell out of there."

"You kissed him and then ran away?"

"Yeah, pretty much."

"Wow." Michelle shook her head. "What'd he do about it?"

"He tried to call a few times. I blocked his number."

"That's pretty cold."

"Hey, whose side are you on here?"

"I have a pre-teen daughter. I watch a lot of Disney movies. I'm on the side of Prince Charming and true love."

"I see," Erin said dryly. "Then you'll be pleased to hear, he showed up a couple days ago and said he wasn't going to give me up without a fight."

"Erin, that is so romantic!"

"And annoying," Erin retorted. "What am I supposed to do with a guy like that?"

"What do you want, an instruction manual? See, when a boy and a girl really, really like each other..."

"It's not gonna work, Shelley."

"Why not?"

"A criminal and a cop? This is more Shakespeare than Disney, Shelley. This is some Romeo and Juliet shit. That's a story that doesn't end with 'they all lived happily ever after.'"

Michelle leaned back in her chair. "Sounds like you've made up your mind. I just have one more question."

"What's that?"

"If you're so sure, why is it still bothering you?"

Erin opened her mouth. She closed it again.

"Well?" Michelle drummed her fingers on the tabletop.

"Because," Erin said. She felt a slow smile form on her face. "Because I want it to work, damn it all. And I do want him."

"You think you can save him? Like Ripper?"

She shook her head. "No. He'll have to save himself." She stood up. "Thanks for the help with the dog, Shelley. I have to go."

Michelle grinned. "You're going for it."

"Shut up."

"Sis, it's a good thing you're a good cop, because you'd be a lousy card player."

"I said, shut up."

"Go on, Erin. I'm cheering for you, remember."

A little laugh burst out of Erin. It was impossible to be mad at Michelle.

"You'll have to let me meet this guy sometime," Michelle said. "He must be something special."

"Yeah. He is."

*   *   *

Erin placed the call on her way home. The phone rang four times. She was trying to decide what she'd say if it went to voicemail when he picked up.

"Evening," Carlyle said.

"Hey. It's me."

"I wasn't sure I'd be hearing from you again," he said.

"Neither was I," she replied. "But I said I'd see you around."

"I'd not forgotten it."

"We need to talk."

"I'm at your disposal."

"Face to face."

"Name the place. I'll find a way to get there."

She smiled to herself. "It's not far. You still remember where I live."

"Aye."

"Be there in an hour."

"My pleasure."

She hung up. At the next stoplight, she looked herself in the eye in the rear-view mirror. The woman who looked back was tired and stressed, but determined. She nodded. She'd avoided this long enough. It was time to have it out.

Chapter 21

Erin spent longer than she should have picking out what to wear. She couldn't decide on comfort versus formality versus attractiveness. If she'd been going out on a date, she'd have gone with her black velvet dress. That was too much. If it were a business meeting, she'd have worn her work blouse and slacks. But that wasn't quite right, either.

Finally, with just a few minutes to spare, she finally dug out her one and only professional skirt. It was a knee-length black pencil skirt. She selected a dark red blouse to go with it. She didn't have time for much makeup, but she dabbed on a little to hide the shadows under her eyes and tied her hair back in her usual ponytail. Rolf watched her preparations with his head resting between his paws. He knew something was up, but not what.

The K-9 heard Carlyle's approach before Erin did, springing to his feet and padding toward the door. Carlyle had apparently gotten past the building's outer door with no trouble at all. Erin wasn't surprised. Guys like him had ways of getting in. She went into the entryway and waited. Her doorbell rang a moment later.

She double-checked the peephole, just in case. For all she knew, those goons who'd tried to tune her up were still out there somewhere. But it was Carlyle. He was wearing a freshly-cleaned dark-gray suit. Instead of his usual dark necktie, he'd opted for burgundy silk. His handsome face was outwardly calm, but she knew him well enough to see the tension just under the surface. He had a brown paper bag in his right hand.

Erin gave it a moment, so he wouldn't know she'd been lurking just inside. Then she took a deep breath and opened the door.

"Evening, Carlyle," she said.

"Evening, Erin."

"C'mon in." She stepped back. He came into the apartment and exchanged a brief glance with Rolf. The Shepherd eyed him coolly, deciding that as long as his partner was okay with the Irishman, so was he. But Rolf kept close to Erin's side as she led the way into the living room.

"You want a drink?" she offered. She'd set out her whiskey and a pair of glasses ahead of time.

He smiled and produced a matching bottle of Glen Docherty-Kinlochewe from the paper bag. "I've come prepared."

"Mine's already open," she said and poured them each a shot. Once she took a seat on her couch, Rolf settled down on his belly. Carlyle sat in her armchair, straight-backed, still tense.

"Relax," Erin said. "I won't bite."

He smiled again. "Forgive me, Erin. I confess, I'm not knowing quite what to expect."

She took a sip of whiskey, welcoming the familiar heat. "It's been a rough few days," she said.

"Successful ones, I gather," he said.

"How do you know that?" she replied. "It's not on the news yet."

"You've an air of the chase about you when you're still in the hunt," he said. "While I'm thinking you're not entirely satisfied, you've a sense of accomplishment, if I don't miss my guess."

"You're right," she said. "We caught him. It was the magician himself. He sabotaged his own magic trick, went up there in front of a whole theater full of people. Can you imagine that? He committed premeditated murder in front of six hundred New Yorkers who were all looking right at him. You know the guts it takes to pull a stunt like that?"

"Perhaps he thought it was so obvious, no one would suspect him," Carlyle said.

"Yeah," Erin said. She laughed quietly. "It took me long enough to tumble to it. His assistant was stealing from him and sleeping with the competition. I think it was the betrayal more than the theft that convinced him to kill her, but does it matter? In the end, it was exactly what it appeared to be. That was the trick. There was no trick. No sneaky angle, no cleverness. He had us chasing our tails."

"That's something of a masterpiece of deceit," he said. "Or would have been, had the lad gotten away with it. It seems he underestimated you."

"And Rolf," she said, reaching down to scratch the dog behind the ears. "This bad boy took a Taser, and it didn't keep him down."

Carlyle nodded. But he still wasn't relaxed. He continued to watch Erin closely, waiting for some sign or signal. That nervousness was very unusual for him.

She met his eyes. "I've been thinking," she said. "About you, and... about us."

"As have I."

"You're so good at angles," she said. "You're always looking ahead, playing everybody, always looking at the long game. I'd always believed you were working an angle. I never figured you might be exactly what you appeared to be. No deception, no cleverness. I thought you were using me, like you use everyone."

She saw the flicker of anger in his eyes and held up a hand, stopping the denial before it crossed his lips. "Both of us have benefited from our working relationship," she went on. "You know it's true. I've closed some tough cases. You got rid of one of your close rivals. Not to mention saving each other's lives a couple of times. I figured that was all there was to it."

"That's how it started," he agreed. "But we did become friends, Erin. And I'm sorry I've damaged that friendship. If I'd known how you'd take it..."

"You wouldn't have kissed me?"

He shook his head. "Darling, I'd have done just the same. I couldn't help myself. I knew the attraction between us was real. I may not be a slave to my passions, like Corky, but I'm not made of stone."

"He came to see me, you know," she said.

"Corky? Why?" Genuine surprise showed on his face.

"He wanted to convince me to give you a chance."

Now Carlyle did look angry. "He'd no right to do that. I'll have words with the lad."

She held up her hand again. "It's okay. He told me... you were mad about me, I think were his words."

His jaw tightened. "Aye," he said quietly. "That's true enough."

"You're too smart not to know what a bad idea this whole thing is," she said.

He nodded and said nothing.

"How would it even work?" she asked. "Would there be O'Malley goons coming out of the woodwork all the time?"

"I've dealt with that situation," he said. "They'll not be troubling you again."

She blinked. "Holy shit," she blurted out. "Did you kill them?"

"Nay, nothing of the sort," he said. "But my lad Ian may have had a bit of a talk with them, convinced them of the error of their ways. I told you, he's the most dangerous lad in this city. You'll perhaps not be surprised he carries a bit of a reputation. There's nothing done to them that won't mend, but they'll not darken your door in the future."

"So that's how this goes? I get in a tough spot, and you send one of your muscle guys to protect me?"

"Aye, Erin, that's how this works," he said, leaning forward. "As far as the O'Malleys are concerned, you're under my protection now. They believe you're working for me, providing information, arresting my rivals, all that manner of thing."

"You let them believe that?" she said with an edge to her voice.

"Aye, since it keeps you safe," he said. He smiled ruefully. "It's an unusual thing, pretending to have an insider with the police. But Evan O'Malley's actually pleased at the prospect. You may recall, his nephew's inside man was arrested some time ago."

"Yeah, I know." She'd been the one to arrest him.

"That puts information from your precinct at a bit of a premium, I think you'd agree. He wants to meet you, Erin."

"Really?" A cold feeling spread through her stomach.

"Aye. That's a good thing, darling. It means he considers you valuable. You're in, Erin. You've nothing to fear from any of my lads, as long as they think you're one of us."

"But I'm not."

"I know that, but they needn't."

"You want me to pretend I'm something I'm not for those jerks?" she retorted.

He shrugged. "I've done it for years."

That made her pause. She wondered, but didn't quite say, Who are you really, Carlyle?

"What about my people?" was what she asked. "What about the NYPD?"

"What about them?" he echoed. "I'll never ask you to do anything against your conscience, darling. I'll not ask you to commit a crime. I can still assist you with your cases, in whatever manner you choose."

"But I have to keep things secret from them," she said.

"You're breaking no laws."

Erin stared at him. "You've thought this through."

"I've thought of little else these past weeks."

"Why?"

"Because I love you."

There it was. The first time he'd said it, and he'd just come right out with it, in his calm, reasonable, conversational voice. But his eyes were soft and open.

"Why?" she said again, and this time there was a little catch in her voice.

"Your spirit, darling. Your passion, your determination, your sheer bloody-minded stubbornness. You've a lovely face, but your heart is lovelier still. I think you're the finest lass I've ever known."

He paused and looked down. "But here's the trouble, Erin. I'm not a good lad to know. I've led a life of trouble and violence. I've done terrible things, and the road I'm on will likely lead me to a churchyard or a jail cell. I do love you, darling, but I'll not ask you to return my feelings."

Erin swallowed. "You're the canniest, cagiest, smartest gangster I've ever met," she said. "And the smoothest son of a bitch I know." Then she smiled at him. "And damned if you don't have the sexiest accent."

He looked up and returned the smile, a little hesitantly. Erin didn't think she'd ever seen him quite so uncertain. "What is it you're wanting from me?" he asked in a near-whisper.

"I'm not asking you to be sorry for what you've done," she said. "I'm asking if you can be better."

"That's a fair request," he said. "Aye, for you, I'm thinking I can be."

She stared into his eyes. "And you've got to promise me something."

"I'm listening."

"Promise me I won't have to put the cuffs on you someday," she said. "Because if you make me arrest you, after all this, I swear to God, I'll kill you."

He didn't blink or look away. "I promise."

"And one other thing."

He raised an eyebrow. "You'll fit right in to my world," he said, his smile broadening. "You're quite skilled at negotiating."

Erin didn't smile. "Promise you'll never lie to me."

"Erin," he said, his own smile vanishing, "I've never lied to you yet, and I'm not about to start. And now I've a question for you."

"Let's hear it."

"How do you feel about me?"

"Damn it, Carlyle," she said. "I can't keep away from you. I'm miserable without you. Don't you know that by now?"

"Aye," he said, and the smile was back on his face. "But I wanted to hear you admit it."

"I tried not to."

"I know." He took her hands in his own. "And I know it's inconvenient."

"Carlyle?" Their faces were only a few inches apart now.

"Aye?"

"You can stop talking now."

It was a slower kiss than their first one. They were gentle with each other, testing, moving carefully. The kiss slowly blossomed and opened. Erin tasted traces of Scotch on his mouth and gently pressed against his lips with the tip of her tongue. He put an arm around her shoulders and drew her closer, sliding onto the couch beside her.

He broke the kiss for a moment. "You're certain of this, darling?" he asked.

"No. Are you?"

He laughed quietly. "The best and worst thing we could possibly do," he said. He kissed her neck just below her ear, making her shiver.

"Can I trust you?" she whispered. Even as she said it, she had her hands on his chest, feeling the lean strength in his body.

"I'd stop bullets for you, darling," he said in an answering whisper. "Though I hope it'll not come to that." He caressed her, her skin tingling at his touch through her blouse.

All their pent-up attraction, all the unacknowledged flirtations, the two months' separation, rose in them. Each explored the other's body with the thrill of discovery, but with a sort of familiarity, too. Erin knew there'd be complications and trouble to come, but here and now, it felt absolutely right. Carlyle's hands and lips seemed to know exactly what to do, bringing her higher with every touch. She met him touch for touch, kiss for kiss. It was a dance of power and danger, like everything about them, but one that was exhilarating and left them breathless, spent and exhausted, entwined in an embrace that felt like nothing could pull apart.

* * *

"This changes everything, doesn't it," Erin said, later.

They were in her bedroom. She'd been lying quietly, enjoying the unfamiliar feeling of sharing her bed with a man. Carlyle had an arm around her shoulders. It felt comfortable, safe. But she knew it wasn't really.

"I've not changed," he said. "I'm the same lad as before. You've just seen me a bit closer."

"Everything else, then," she said.

"That's as may be. You're still a damned fine copper."

"And you're still a gangster."

"A gangster who loves you."

She shivered, but not from the cold. "You think that'll be enough?"

He kissed her cheek and drew her closer. "I think if it weren't true, nothing would be enough."

Erin turned to face him. "What, so now you're sweet-talking me?"

He smiled. "Is it working?"

"I believe you," she said. "Yeah, I guess it's working. If it's a trick, it's a pretty good one."

"You said it yourself," he said. "The cleverest trick is when there's no trick at all."

"So you're a magician, too?"

"Oh, aye. It's like that lad Sinatra sings. That old black magic has me in its spell."

Erin raised an eyebrow. "I wouldn't have taken you for a Sinatra fan."

"Why not?" Carlyle replied. "The lad was connected. He always got on well with those in the life."

She shook her head. "I have to tell you, I don't know how we're going to work this out. I'm not sure this was a good idea."

Carlyle smiled gently. "I've no regrets, darling. And I've no intention of letting you go. Whatever happens, it'll happen to the both of us. It's that old black magic called love."

Here's a sneak peek from Book 7: Death by Chocolate

Coming Winter 2019

Vic Neshenko took careful aim. Like the good rifleman he was, he knew not to rush his shot. He breathed in, held it a moment, and let the breath out slowly. Then, in that instant of perfect stillness, he took the shot.

The crumpled piece of paper ricocheted off the rim of the garbage can and bounced onto the floor of the Precinct 8 Major Crimes office.

Vic groaned and sagged in his chair.

"That's game," Erin O'Reilly said. "Five to four. Next case we close, you're buying the first round."

Erin's partner Rolf let out a long, slow sigh. He lay on the floor next to her desk, on a square of sample carpet. The German Shepherd had his snout between his paws. His eyes were half-closed and unfocused. It was a slow, sleepy Saturday afternoon.

Lieutenant Webb, their commanding officer, twirled a cigarette between his fingers. They were in a public New York facility, so of course smoking wasn't allowed, and the cig wasn't lit. He clearly wished it was.

"Will someone, for God's sake, get murdered?" Vic asked the ceiling. "I'm bored out of my skull."

"I think New York's seen enough people murdered in the name of God," Webb said dryly. "We've had our fill of terrorists."

"Murder's usually more personal," Erin added.

"I'd take it personal," Vic said, "if anyone murdered me."

"How're your fives coming along?" Webb asked Erin.

"Just about done."

Webb was talking about the DD-5, an infamous piece of NYPD paperwork used to add detail to a complaint report. "If it's not on a five, it didn't happen," was a common phrase in Erin's old precinct down in Queens. Filling one out wasn't her favorite use of an afternoon.

"It's okay to admit you're just looking at porn," Vic said.

"Okay, you caught me," she said, putting up her hands. "Sergeant Brown pointed me at this great website. It's got these Russian girls on it. There's one here who looks kind of like your mom."

Vic gave her a false smile and showed her one of his fingers.

"Three days after Valentine's Day," Webb said, leaning back in his chair. "And love is still in the air."

"What'd you do for the holiday?" Erin asked Vic.

"I drank. Alone."

"That reminds me," Webb said. "My alimony's coming due. I better get a check in the mail."

"How about you, Erin?" Vic asked. "You have any lights and sirens last night?"

"Wouldn't you love to know."

"I would, actually," he said. "It'd give me a nice, warm image to get me through February. It's a Russian month. Dark, cold, nothing to do but drink."

"And March is like February's hangover," Webb said.

"C'mon, Erin," Vic said. "At least one of us gold shields oughta be getting some. I know I didn't get laid, and the Lieutenant, well, just look at him. So that leaves you. Did you take one for the team?"

Erin shook her head. "I'll never talk."

"I knew it!" Vic said triumphantly. "I'm thinking drunken hookup at that Irish bar she hangs out at."

"The one full of wise guys?" Webb asked.

At that moment, Webb's phone rang. Erin felt a rush of relief as the lieutenant took the call. Her fellow detectives had been getting a little too close to the mark. She had been with someone on Valentine's Day, and it was a man they definitely wouldn't approve of.

"Your prayers are answered," Webb announced, standing up. "We got a body."

Vic jumped to his feet. "Now that's what I'm talking about."

Rolf, catching the sudden energy in the room, scrambled to his feet and looked expectantly at Erin. She grabbed his leash and clipped it to his collar. "Where we going, sir?" she asked Webb.

"Dentist's office," he said, deadpan.

Vic's shoulders slumped. "I knew it was too good to be true."

*   *   *

The dentist was in Greenwich Village, in a building overlooking Washington Square Park. Erin parked her Dodge

Charger next to a pair of squad cars and the coroner's van. Vic and Webb were close behind in their Taurus.

"Looks like we're late," Vic muttered. "Maybe they'll at least have some good magazines in the waiting room."

"I doubt it," Erin said. "I mean, it's usually *Good Housekeeping, Better Homes and Gardens,* maybe *Seventeen* or *Cosmo.* What sort of thing do you read?"

Vic shrugged. "*Guns and Ammo. Soldier of Fortune.*"

"Surprised?" Webb asked Erin.

It was her turn to shrug. "Mostly, I'm just surprised he knows how to read."

They showed their shields to a uniformed officer in the lobby and took the elevator to the sixth floor. Another uniform was guarding a door labeled "Norman Ridgeway, DDS."

"That's our victim?" Erin asked.

"We'll see in a minute," Webb said. "Dispatch just told me we had a sudden death."

"Must've been suspicious for them to call in Major Crimes right away," Vic said.

"They called it a probable homicide," Webb said.

The waiting room was populated by two patients, an oral hygienist, and a secretary. The hygienist was sniffling into a tissue. One patient was a young man, college age, who was leafing through a back issue of *People* magazine. The other was a thirtysomething businesswoman who looked pissed off.

"The victim's in his office," the cop at the door offered, pointing past the front desk.

"Excuse me," the businesswoman said, standing up. "I don't know who you think you are, but I've been waiting here almost forty-five minutes. This is totally unacceptable."

"I'm Lieutenant Webb," Webb said. "Major Crimes. We'll need a statement from you, but I hope you won't be inconvenienced much longer."

The woman made an exasperated sound in her nose. "I don't see how this day could possibly get any worse."

"You could've been the victim instead of a witness," Vic offered. "That'd probably be worse."

She glared at him. He gave her his best meeting-the-public smile and moved on.

Erin steered Rolf past the bystanders to the office. She'd been a cop almost twelve years. She'd responded to gruesome traffic accidents, homicides, suicides, and found bodies that had been dead for days by the time they were reported. Her last big, dramatic case had featured a victim literally sawn in half with a spectacular amount of blood spray. She was ready for anything.

It was an anticlimax. The victim was sprawled on a leather couch against his office wall. He didn't have a mark on him. His lips were tinged blue, and there were flecks of foam at the corners of his mouth, but otherwise, he didn't look half bad. There was one odd thing about the body, however.

"Where's his clothes?" she asked aloud.

"The paramedics reported the body was this way when they arrived," a woman said. She was wearing a white lab coat and disposable gloves, and was kneeling beside the naked corpse.

"Hi, Levine," Erin said, recognizing the medical examiner for their precinct.

"Hey, doc," Vic said, coming up behind Erin. "He's dead, but I bet his teeth are in fantastic condition."

Sarah Levine blinked. "I haven't examined his dentition," she said. "When there's no question of positive identification of the victim, it's not a priority."

"You have a preliminary COD?" Webb asked, moving past his detectives into the room.

"Discoloration of the lips and fingernails," Levine said. "Cyanosis, typical of asphyxia. The lack of ligature marks on the throat indicates a probable chemical cause. The most likely agent is cyanide, but I'll have to do bloodwork to be certain."

Erin glanced around the room. She saw a desk with a computer on it, an office chair behind the desk, and a coffee table. On the table was an open candy box.

"Happy Valentine's Day," she murmured.

Webb and Vic followed her look. "I wouldn't eat those," Webb said. "I'm guessing they might kill you."

"And give you cavities," Vic added.

Levine leaned forward and carefully parted the corpse's lips with a pair of gloved fingers. "Trace amounts of a brown substance between the canines and lodged in the molars," she announced. "This supports the hypothesis of toxic candy."

"I told you to check the teeth," Vic said triumphantly.

"So," Erin said. "Who was in here with him?"

"Maybe he liked eating chocolate alone," Vic said.

"Naked?" Webb asked, raising an eyebrow.

"Hey, this is New York City," Vic said. "We got all types here."

"Given the options in the waiting room," Erin said, "I'm guessing the oral hygienist."

"Not the skirt with the bad attitude?" Webb asked.

"I'm thinking the one who's crying is more likely," she replied.

He sighed. "Okay, we better talk to her."

* * *

They didn't want to take statements in the office with the dead guy, or in front of the other witnesses, so they ended up using one of the examining rooms. Erin thought it was a little weird to be interviewing a person of interest who was sitting in a dental chair, but it was hardly the strangest thing she'd done in her twelve years with the NYPD.

The hygienist, a pretty blonde named Amber Hayward, carried a crumpled tissue in one hand. She kept dabbing at her eyes with it. Her mascara was running.

"Miss Hayward," Webb said, "can you tell us what happened?"

"I came in to work," Amber said. "Well, I had breakfast before that. And before that, I put on my makeup. And my clothes. And got out of bed. I guess I woke up first."

"Take your time," Webb said.

"The first appointment was at nine," she went on. "That was Mr. Pavlicek, with his root canal. It was the number nineteen molar. Doctor Ridgeway decided to do a standard procedure, with..."

Webb held up a hand. "I don't think we need the details of the procedure," he said. "Maybe you could skip ahead a little."

Amber nodded. "After Mr. Pavlicek, we had three more appointments. Teddy Coogan, extraction of a dead baby tooth, 5D. Then Paul Dexter, impacted wisdom tooth, number sixteen. And Lori Smithers, routine exam and cleaning, just before lunch."

"Does anyone else work in the office?" Webb asked.

"Valerie Booker, our other hygienist," Amber said. "And Della Ackerman, our secretary."

"Where's Valerie?" Vic asked.

"Out to lunch," Amber said. "She'll be back any minute. Oh God, what am I going to tell her?" She blew her nose loudly.

"What happened at lunchtime?" Webb asked.

"We had an hour and a half blocked out on the schedule," she said. "Valerie went to meet her mom. Mrs. Booker works for a Wall Street firm. They have lunch together once a week.

Norm... Doctor Ridgeway, I mean... he said we'd have time to eat... later."

"Miss Hayward," Webb said quietly, "were you and Doctor Ridgeway physically intimate?"

Amber nodded and whimpered.

"Amber," Erin said. "Where did the chocolates come from?"

The hygienist's eyes filled with new tears. "I gave them to him!" she wailed. "I put... I put one... right in his mouth! I killed him! Oh God, I killed him!"

"Well, this'll be a short case," Vic whispered in Erin's ear.

She ignored him. "Amber," she asked the young woman, "was the box opened?"

"What?" Amber sniffled.

"When you went to give Doctor Ridgeway the chocolates, had the box been opened previously?"

"I... I don't understand."

Erin knew it was important to be patient when interviewing witnesses. "Was the box wrapped? With plastic?"

"Oh. No."

"Were any chocolates missing, or disturbed?"

"Yes," Amber said. "It wasn't a full box. Maybe four or five were missing. Rocky said he ate a few. It's so typical of him. Even a gift, he just can't help himself."

"Who's Rocky?" Webb asked sharply.

"Rocky Nicoletti," she said. "My... my boyfriend."

Webb's eyebrows went up. "Your boyfriend," he echoed in a flat voice.

She nodded. Then a thought hit her. "Oh my God. He might have eaten... he might be... oh God. Rocky!" Then she started crying again.

Erin exchanged glances with Vic. He shrugged. Rolf, at Erin's side, was the only one who didn't look surprised. To him, all these human interactions were equally nonsensical. He kept watching his partner, in case she decided to do something more interesting.

"Miss Hayward," Webb said. "Were you and Doctor Ridgeway getting along?"

"Wha... what?" she snuffled.

"Had you been fighting?" he asked gently. "Was he putting pressure on you to do something you didn't want to?"

Amber shook her head. "No! Norm... Norm's a sweetheart. He's kind and... and good with kids. He talked about dinosaurs with Teddy Coogan!"

"So you weren't angry at him?" Webb pressed.

Erin saw recognition hit Amber. "You think I wanted to hurt him?" Amber exclaimed. "You think I took a box of chocolates, and... and poisoned them... and gave one... to my Normie?"

"Normie?" Vic said, but he said it quietly and no one took any notice of him.

"You..." Amber advanced on Webb, waving her used tissue in his face. "You... you big jerk!" She threw the soggy scrap of paper at him. It bounced off his trench coat and landed on the carpet. Then Amber buried her face in her hands and sobbed.

Webb didn't react. He'd been called much worse.

"Amber," Erin said gently. "Rocky gave you the chocolates?"

It took a moment to get through to her, and she had to repeat the question, but the other woman finally nodded.

"Were they a Valentine's Day gift?" Erin asked.

Amber nodded again.

"Amber," she said. "Please listen. This is important. Did Rocky know about Normie?"

"I... I don't... I don't know," Amber managed to say between hiccupping sobs. Then she lost whatever was left of her self-control and became useless from a police perspective.

Erin cocked her head to Webb and Vic. They stepped into the hallway just outside the examining room.

"What do you think?" Webb asked his two detectives.

"If she's a murderer," Vic said, "I'll field-strip my gun and eat it, one piece at a time."

"I'm with Vic," Erin said. "I don't even think Ridgeway was the intended target."

"It does seem like a pretty iffy way to kill someone," Webb said. "You think it was meant for Miss Hayward?"

Erin nodded. "If she's telling the truth, and Rocky gave them to her..."

"Then Rocky's got some explaining to do," Vic finished for her.

Ready for more?

Join Steven Henry's author email list
for the latest on new releases, upcoming books and
series, behind-the-scenes details, events, and more.

Be the first to know about new releases in the Erin
O'Reilly Mysteries by signing up at
tinyurl.com/StevenHenryEmail

About the Author

Steven Henry learned how to read almost before he learned how to walk. Ever since he began reading stories, he wanted to put his own on the page. He lives a very quiet and ordinary life in Minnesota with his wife and dog.

Also by Steven Henry

Ember of Dreams
The Clarion Chronicles, Book One

When magic awakens a long-forgotten folk, a noble lady, a young apprentice, and a solitary blacksmith band together to prevent war and seek understanding between humans and elves.

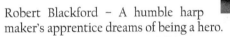

Lady Kristyn Tremayne – An otherwise unremarkable young lady's open heart and inquisitive mind reveal a hidden world of magic.

Robert Blackford – A humble harp maker's apprentice dreams of being a hero.

Master Gabriel Zane – A master blacksmith's pursuit of perfection leads him to craft an enchanted sword, drawing him out of his isolation and far from his cozy home.

Lord Luthor Carnarvon – A lonely nobleman with a dark past has won the heart of Kristyn's mother, but at what cost?

Readers love *Ember of Dreams*

"The more I got to know the characters, the more I liked them. The female lead in particular is a treat to accompany on her journey from ordinary to extraordinary."

"The author's deep understanding of his protagonists' motivations and keen eye for psychological detail make Robert and his companions a likable and memorable cast."

Learn more at tinyurl.com/emberofdreams.

More great titles from Clickworks Press

www.clickworkspress.com

The Altered Wake
Megan Morgan

Amid growing unrest, a family secret and an ancient laboratory unleash long-hidden superhuman abilities. Now newly-promoted Sentinel Cameron Kardell must chase down a rogue superhuman who holds the key to the powers' origin: the greatest threat Cotarion has seen in centuries – and Cam's best friend.

"Incredible. Starts out gripping and keeps getting better."

Learn more at clickworkspress.com/sentinel1.

Hubris Towers: The Complete First Season
Ben Y. Faroe & Bill Hoard

Comedy of manners meets comedy of errors in a new series for fans of Fawlty Towers and P. G. Wodehouse.

"So funny and endearing"

"Had me laughing so hard that I had to put it down to catch my breath"

"Astoundingly, outrageously funny!"

Learn more at clickworkspress.com/hts01.

Death's Dream Kingdom
Gabriel Blanchard

A young woman of Victorian London has been transformed into a vampire. Can she survive the world of the immortal dead— or perhaps, escape it?

"The wit and humor are as Victorian as the setting... a winsomely vulnerable and tremendously crafted work of art."

"A dramatic, engaging novel which explores themes of death, love, damnation, and redemption."

Learn more at clickworkspress.com/ddk.

Share the love!

Join our microlending team at
kiva.org/team/clickworkspress.

Keep in touch!

Join the Clickworks Press email list
and get freebies, production updates, special deals,
behind-the-scenes sneak peeks, and more.

Sign up today at clickworkspress.com/join.